I Am A Worshiper

Discovering My Identity In the Throne Room of God's Presence

Cheryl Salem

Unless otherwise indicated, all Scripture quotations are taken from the *New King James® Bible.* Copyright © 1982 by Thomas Nelson, Inc. Used by permission.

Sixth Printing

I Am A Worshiper

ISBN 1-890370-33-9

Printed in United States of America

Salem Family Ministries
PO Box 1595
Cathedral City, CA 92234

www.salemfamilyministries.org

Disclaimer: The views expressed in this book contain my personal opinions and experiences throughout my life and time spent in God's presence. I express them as my opinion and view only, and share them with you from my personal lifelong experience from my heart. I am only communicating what has worked for me personally, and what I have personally experienced with the Lord.

Contents

Acknowledgements

The Lord knows me better than I know myself and He knows I need help and lots of it. I need help every day of my life and my precious husband has given me more support and encouragement than any one person could ever hope for. Thank you my beloved husband, Harry Salem, for your love, support, and ability to finish all the many things I seem to start in our ministry and lives together!

In this particular book I was pushing a deadline to get it to the printers and as usual, Debbie Squire, our dear and precious friend and co-laborer in this ministry, allowed me to push her week after week to complete this on time. Debbie, you did a great job with the cover and the layout, and so many more detailed things you do to make all of these projects seem seamless and effortless. You are a great gift to all of our family and especially me!

I solicited help for proof-reading and editing and asked for it to be back to me 'yesterday' each time I sent it out to friends to help me get the manuscript ready. I want to send a special thank you to Thom and Kathy Rabey, Kathy Eberhart, and Kim Huey for the careful eye to detail you all gave me these last few weeks. Thank you for your efforts and tireless reading and re-reading of this book. You are all true worshipers of God and that's why I knew you would be the best to help me finish this.

And last, a huge thank you to our daily intercessors in this ministry who stand in the gap and pray for us in all our ministry assignments. Because of your prayers we are finishing strong in the name of Jesus and the power of the Holy Spirit. Thank you!

Introduction

I AM a worshiper. I have settled and sealed my true identity within the realm of living in Christ. You can too! Your life will change when you stop the wrestling between your natural self (flesh) and your supernatural identity (spirit) within you. You may be housed in flesh but YOU ARE NOT FLESH! You are spirit and we worship God in spirit and truth. (John 4)

We don't worship in flesh, and for those who try to do this, it is not worship at all, but merely some form of human performance. We can't perform for God. He knows us; He knows who He has made us to be. When we are trying to be anything or anyone other than the DNA code written by Almighty God, then we are failing in all possible directions.

Don't let the devil rewrite your DNA code within you. God knew who you were before you were ever in your mother's womb. He made you, created you, programmed you, and coded you. Whatever term helps you understand better that God has designed you from the very core of your cellular level as a worshiper of the most-high God, then that's the one I want you to meditate on day and night until it is sealed and settled within you.

God coded your identity within the very DNA of you. There is no one else in the whole world like you nor will there ever be another one just like you. God set your tone, your frequency, your sound, and your worship in place before you ever left the realm of the throne room of heaven. He knows you. HE KNOWS YOU!

You may not know who you really are yet, but you are not a mystery to the King of kings. He knows you, because He created you to worship Him! You have been sent on assignment to the realm of earth to make His praise glorious.

Your life situations or circumstances, what family you were born into or environment you were reared in have no bearing on whom you really are. Your identity is sealed and settled in the realm of heaven and your earth assignment if you choose to accept it, (to quote Mission Impossible!) is to discover who you really are and never ever hold back again the sound of worship that is within you! You are to make that sound, never fear or be intimidated, for the Lord of lords forever!

You are not to judge your sound, or your talent. Your talent or gifting or personality is not what qualifies you to be a worshiper of God. Your DNA within the depths of your cellular level is what qualifies you! God qualified you, approved you, and accepted you before you were in your mother's womb! I keep saying this because I want you to understand before we dive into the depths of your being, that you were who you are, before you were planted within the womb of your earthly mother. Before your mom and dad ever got together and sperm found egg, GOD KNEW YOU!

Your parents did not make you; God made you. He made you for His glory. He made you for praise and worship! He made you to give back to Him the sound that He has given you.

So let's stop trying to do things on our own anymore. I want you to stop trying to be a better you. I want you to stop trying to sound like someone else, or be someone else. I want you to get comfortable being you!

I don't have to try to be Cheryl. I am Cheryl. I don't have to work at being me, because I am totally at home being myself. When I am trying to be something or someone other than who I really am, it's work! It's hard work, and generally I fail miserably.

I was created to be me, but not just any *me*. I was created to be a worshiper of the most-high God. My sound is His sound; the tones of His throne room are coded within my very DNA. Trying to sound like another singer, or move like them, or dress like them, or act like them is exactly that, an act! Stop it. Be you. You are perfect just the way you were made from your mother's womb.

You are not the collective parts of your mother and father's combined DNA. You are the collective parts and instruments, sounds, and movements of your Father God who made you and knew you EVEN BEFORE YOUR MOTHER'S WOMB. Your Father is God! He made you. He designed you for greatness. When you try to be anything or anyone other than your God given design, you are trying to dumb yourself down to a much lower level, even a copy of someone else!

The scripture says in Revelation 4 to '*Come up higher.*' Don't stay down low in a place of lower slower thinking and being. You live and breathe and have your being hidden inside Christ! Let's discover this together, and settle it forever. Until you have settled who you were created to be and until you are doing what you were created to do, your life will be an inner wrestling match. It's time for your supernatural spirit to win over your earthly flesh!

You are a super hero in the kingdom of God! Maybe you didn't know that but you are! You are called and appointed and anointed for such a time as this. Your sound is valuable and important to the pulling down of strongholds. Until you settle this, demonic powers will rule where they should be shattered by your worship!

You are born to win! You are born to change the world! You are a child of the King, a true king's kid! Yep, that's you. You are not a loser. You are a finisher with the 'Ti' sound within your coded signature. (If you are uncertain of what this means you need to read *Tones of the Throne Room*! Do-Re-Mi-Fa-Sol-La-Ti!) God wants an intimate relationship with you and it is not the Father God who is standing far away!

Once you know who you really are, nothing can stop you from fulfilling your purpose and plan set forth by your Creator! It matters not what others have said about you, or to you, in trying to redefine your identity. The only power within your life of words spoken to you, are those words you have given power to by believing! No person, situation, circumstance, or life event has a right to your identity.

Before you have finished the last page of this book you will be able to make every negative word spoken to you about your identity become null and void without power of fulfillment! As you read through these chapters ask the Holy Spirit to bring to your remembrance words that have affected the way you feel about yourself, and words that have affected who you think you are. As He brings those words, thoughts, and phrases to your head, I want you to turn to the back of the book and start jotting them down. No matter how negative or hurtful they are, please just jot them down. When you complete this book, we are going to tear that page out and annihilate every word!

Are you properly intrigued and motivated to want to be changed into the very image of Christ? Then let's go for it and settle and seal your identity as a worshiper forever! YOU ARE A WORSHIPER OF THE MOST-HIGH GOD!

Chapter One
Love Identity

I must know who I am, to be a true worshiper of God with my identity in place. So must you. The Bible tells us early in scripture, in Genesis 1:26, that the Father, Son, and Holy Spirit made mankind in Their image, in the image and likeness of the Godhead He made all mankind. That means that you and I are made in His image. You are not the exception to God's plan and God's word.

You are made in His image. You are not the image of your parents, or your life's situation, or your circumstances. You are not the image of words spoken over you all your life. You are the very image of the triune Godhead.

How do I know this to be true? Because the Bible is true and if this statement in Genesis is not true, then I can't believe any other word in the Bible. Neither can you! So decide right now for yourself in whose image are you made? God made you in His image!

The Amplified Bible reads this way for verses 26-27.

"God said, Let Us [Father, Son, and Holy Spirit] make mankind in Our image, after Our likeness, and let them have complete authority over the fish of the sea, the birds of the air, the [tame] beasts, and over all the earth, and over everything that creeps upon the earth. So God created man in His own image, in the image and likeness of God He created him; male and female He created them."

Knowing that you were made in God's image should help you understand your position and power upon the earth. God is a creator by nature, and so much more! He has more attributes than we will ever be able to discover after 100,000 years in His glorious throne room. But we can know for sure those attributes that are spelled out within the scriptures and also those we know of Him through our personal experience and journey while here on earth.

The truth in the above scripture is that we are made like Him. We are made, created in His image, looking like a mirror reflection of who He is. Once you realize this amazing truth, you will stop speaking evil of God's image when you speak and think of yourself! You are God's image; stop speaking evil about God's image! That's you!

You must learn to rehearse what God says about you and stop replaying in your mind's memory what others, including yourself, have said about you. Your identity is not supposed to be set by the sound waves of other people or even by your own sounds spoken over you. Your identity is set even before you were in your mother's womb. You are made in God's image; you are His image on the earth!

The catch to this entire equation lies in you 'knowing' your Creator. You can never emulate, or imitate, or reflect whom you don't know. The intricacies and details of the one being imitated are vital to the success of the copy! Without knowing God intimately, we can never be successful in our quest to be like Him.

God made you in His image, not because He needed you, but because He wants you. He so adores and loves us that we were made in His image because of His deep love for us. I believe that He is the ultimate parent. When a baby is born into a family the scrutiny begins. This is really fresh in my mind because our first grandbaby girl, Mia Gabrielle, has just recently been born as I am writing this chapter.

She is just weeks old, and every day (yes I said everyday!), we go to Roman and Stephanie's home to have our time with Mia Gabrielle. We look carefully at everything, from her toes to her ears.

We search her little face and body for anything that is similar to our own. She has my big toe and the color of my eyes and I am forever thrilled! She has my narrow feet and she can smile with one side of her face, all just like me!

Papa Salem has his own discoveries of similarities to him. Uncle Harry has his discoveries, and of course, Roman and Stephanie, and her parents and family all have their discoveries!

What is so amazing about all of this is we just want her to look like us, in some ways and parts! We may not even like ourselves, but we sure do want her, this perfect and precious one, to be like us!

Can you imagine if we are so consumed with this search for any similarities, how much more the Father searches our lives, hearts, minds, and our very beings, for any similarities to Him? He made us like Him!

Everything within us is like Him. Everything on the outside is like Him! Our sound is His sound! He adores us; He loves us. We were made completely and totally with a 'love identity'!

Jesus told us in Matthew 22:37-38, "*Jesus said to him, 'You shall love the Lord your God with all your heart, with all your soul, and with all your mind. This is the first commandment. And the second is like it. You shall love your neighbor as yourself.'*"

Because He made us in love, He wants us to reciprocate on our own accord, as our own choice, to love Him first and foremost, above anything and everything else! Until we learn how to wholeheartedly love the Lord our God, we will not be successful in who we are for His glory. The success of fulfilling our God identity of love is in our choice to love Him first!

Jesus plainly states that loving God is our first priority, and the second is to love others. It is easy to see that we cannot love others until we learn to truly love God in the deepest of intimacy possible. These two things are very close on the list of first and second.

Sometimes I believe we get confused and think that when we love others then we love Him. And in some cases, it is because we love Him that we have the power and ability to love others. Especially when we are trying to love those who are so very hard to love, then I am certain we love the unlovely because of the deep 'first love' we have for Him.

But we must never replace our secret time of being 'in love' with Him with our need to do and please others. Our first love, our first place, our first thing, first, first, first . . . must be our chosen love for Him and Him alone. We were created for intimacy with Him. The human race was created by God to simply 'be' with Him. He adores us. We don't deserve this adoration, but He adores us anyway.

Loving God is not as easy as one might think. Oh, don't misunderstand me here. God is easy to love; God *is* love! It's not on His part that loving God is difficult. It's within our human part that loving God becomes difficult. Because of human 'sin' nature we are self focused, self seeking, self protecting, and well, yes, self, self, self. People now have more 'selfies' on their phones than they do pictures of others and scenery. We are a 'self centered' bunch of folks!

This generation is so self focused that Webster's Dictionary has had to add a word to their dictionary, 'Selfie'. Yes, this generation is a total embodiment of the fulfillment of 2 Timothy 3:1-7, "*But know this, that in the last days perilous times will come:*
For men will be lovers of themselves, lovers of money, boasters, proud, blasphemers, disobedient to parents, unthankful, unholy,
unloving, unforgiving, slanderers, without self-control, brutal, despisers of good,
traitors, headstrong, haughty, lovers of pleasure rather than lovers of God,
having a form of godliness but denying its power. And from such people turn away!
For of this sort are those who creep into households and make captives of gullible women loaded down with sins, led away by various lusts,
always learning and never able to come to the knowledge of the truth."

Yes, that just about sums up this generation. And the Bible says to stay away from people like that! Then you will have a short list of people you can call friends, but you will know they are true godly friends when they don't fulfill the list above from 2 Timothy.

We are incapable of truly loving God the way He deserves to be loved until we abandon 'self' and become all about Him. And the catch is that it is impossible to abandon self without a willful decision to seek Him, serve Him, and love Him with all our hearts!

It's not easy to do what Jesus is commanding here! But it is vital if we are to truly become His image on the earth and fulfill our destiny and walk out the very sounds of our DNA that God Himself coded within us!

Your first love coded into your DNA is not self-preservation. Your first love is to love the Lord your God with all your heart, mind, and soul. This is not a suggestion. This is a commandment. Until we learn how to fulfill this first commandment, there is no need to try and move out into the rest of the list! First things must be first with God, and this is a commandment from the throne room of heaven!

We must discipline ourselves to keep first things first in our lives. It is much easier to 'do' than to 'be'. And yet God has made it very clear that loving Him with all three levels of our being, outer court, inner court, and holy of holies of whom we really are, is imperative if we are to be His image and discover our true identities. Our 'love identity' must be established and brought to the forefront of our being before we can move on to discover more of the depths of who God has created us to be.

We are created similar in architecture to the temple, with three levels of intimacy. The outer court is learning to discipline our physical flesh lives to love God, and overcome our flesh and be led by the Spirit of God. Romans 8:4 states, "*For as many as are led by the Spirit of God, they are the sons of God.*"

To be a 'son of God' means a level of being His image, in His likeness. A son looks like, and acts like his father. We act like our Father God when His Spirit leads us. We must know Him and be intimate with Him, to be led by His Spirit! We must develop a deep trust of the Spirit of God to allow Him to lead us!

Don't get discouraged! We have only begun a journey into the intimacies of who He is, and ultimately who we are. It's a journey and a lifetime one at that!

This is a stripping away of layers of flesh first, which is the (outer court). Then the soul realm follows, which includes the mind, the will, and the emotions, (the inner court). Then ultimately we find the holy of holies, which helps us deal with the discoveries of our true identity as we discover His true identity!

Intimacy is slow, deliberate, and sometimes painful, as we turn loose of those things that we thought were protecting us from more hurt and deeper betrayal. Two years ago, I was in prayer one morning and the Holy Spirit said to me, "You have done life backwards all of your life." I was somewhat confused, thinking that He was speaking a mystery to me, or something that I was trying to make much more complicated than what He was really saying.

I could not put all the pieces together in my mind and finally I simply said, "What? I don't understand what You are saying." Again, the Spirit of God repeated the same words. "You have done life backwards all of your life."

I meditated on the statement for quite a while when finally I said, "Lord, I must be low and slow today because I don't understand. Will you please elaborate and explain to me what I have done backwards?"

He said, "You have loved Me, and trusted people. I never asked you to do that. I asked you to trust Me, and love people. Because you have done this backwards all your life, you have been in a continual place of turmoil and pain. People will hurt you when you trust them. People are innately not trustworthy."

"I am all together trustworthy and yet you don't trust Me to the level I require of you to be intimately acquainted with Me. Until you learn to trust Me completely, you can never love people to the level they must be loved to cover the sins of their lives in and towards you."

Immediately I was flooded with so many scriptures in my mind. I remembered, 1 Peter 4:8, "*Above all things have intense and unfailing love for one another, for love covers a multitude of sins [forgives and disregards the offenses of others].* (AMP) I had totally missed the true meaning until that moment of revelation. 1 Corinthians 13 began to flood my memory also.

"Love suffers long and is kind; love does not envy; love does not parade itself, it is not puffed up; love does not behave rudely; love does not seek its own; love is not provoked; love thinks no evil; love does not rejoice in iniquity; love rejoices in the truth; love bears all things; love believes all things; love hopes all things, love endures all things; love never fails."

How little true love had I walked in all my life because I trusted people instead of loving people? I said to the Lord, "I see the truth now, Lord! I must only trust You, and when I can truly trust You, then I have the capacity to love people!" This revelation has changed my heart, and has helped me not get hurt over and over by people who are innately not trustworthy. Typically people, in general, are self-serving.

What is my place? Do I try to correct, fix, teach, and help those? Nope, I have one job to do for all people. I must love them! With the Lord's help, and the more intimately acquainted I am with the One who is only LOVE, I am equipped to love people, all people. I am able through Christ to love those who are easy to love and those who are very hard to love.

It is not about them, but about me, and how deeply I can lose my self-identity and walk in my God identity as a worshiper of Him! When I know who I am, then I can be who I am created to be!

My first love cannot be me. My first love must be Him, and Him only. When we learn to love God abandoned of self, then, we can truly walk in His first commandment. I shall love the Lord my God with all my heart, mind, and soul!

This is the first commandment and I will obey it. How can you try to obey anything else the Spirit of God tells you, if you have not mastered the first commandment to love Him with your entire being! He deserves this kind of abandoned love, and you need to love Him this way desperately.

You are a worshiper of God, but you cannot truly worship Him, until you truly, with all your being, love Him! You will not trust whom you do not love; you will not obey whom you do not trust.

Knowing that you must spend a lifetime learning to allow the Holy Spirit to teach you how to love the Lover of your soul is vital. This is a journey, not a sprint, with the Lover of your soul. We will learn more every day. We will have periods of great success in this journey and then we will get really busy in life and neglect our heavenly Lover.

We will lose focus of who is our first love and we will feel horrible and have to start all over in this journey. Yes, everyone does this. That is why we have the precious scripture in 1 John 1:9, "*If we confess our sins, He is faithful and just to forgive us our sins and to cleanse us from all unrighteousness."*

This scripture is not written for the unbeliever but for the believer who, along the journey, gets off and has to have a way back in to His presence. Repentance and confession are the ways back into the intimate journey of learning to love Him more. Making and keeping Him, as our first love, is a lifetime commitment and journey. We don't always do it right.

In our humanness, it is easier to 'do' than to 'be'. Works are easier than love. The children of Israel gave us a clear depiction of that as they journeyed in the wilderness, begging Moses to go to God and get a set of rules to live by, since they felt much as we do today, that rules are easier than being led by the Holy Spirit on a minute by minute basis.

But God created us to commune with Him, to walk and talk and be with Him. When we stay in our rightful place, then we can walk out our love identity and seal and settle who we are forever.

Understanding that the three levels of intimacy with our Father as we learn to love Him in the outer court, inner court, and holy of holies of our personal lives also apply to other people as well. Remember that the Holy Spirit told me to love people but not to trust people? I am to trust God and love people, not the other way around.

As you walk this earth walk with other people in your life, you will learn to keep people in their correct circle also. People who are the most trustworthy (never to the level of the Lord but more trustworthy than the casual friendship) may have access on occasion to the holy of holies of your life. But this is a very small group and it may change daily. When people prove to you that they cannot be trusted to this level of intimacy with you, you simply in your heart move them out further from your holy of holies.

You don't have to tell them what level they are in! Absolutely not! Don't be so quick to share everything with everybody. Protect yourself, your heart, and remember your holy of holies place is made for your love relationship with the King of kings and Lord of lords, for the very Lover of your soul. So don't just let anybody and everybody in there!

You have three circles of relationships (outer circle, inner circle, and holy of holies). In the case with most people, they will always be in your outer circle. They may not have to know their position, but you know where they are. They are too far from your heart to really hurt you. They don't have 'your ear' and their movements don't alert your eyes to always be watching them. They are distracting if you allow them to be too close. You love them deeply but you don't trust them. They have not earned that trust and they may never earn that trust.

Then there are those you have known a very long time. You can allow them into your inner circle. You can trust them to know you without judging you. They can be around you in a more intimate way without fear of them shooting you with arrows of hurt filled words.

Then there is the holy of holies of your life with people. Very few people ever have access here, for this is reserved for the deepest of trust and love. The only one who can truly be trusted to be here is your Holy God.

But we long to have people in our holy of holies with 'skin on them', so we allow a few along the way of life's journey, only to put them back over and over again in the inner circle. It's a journey; don't beat yourself up over this. The Holy

Spirit will guide you, teach you, and love you through all these human (people) relationships. And He will teach you all things! Trust Him completely! Keep your first love in place.

To be a child of God you must work out the deepest part of your broken self-identity. Digging inside your own broken places does not heal you. You become healed by studying the depth and height of the immeasurable love inside the One who made you in His image. So stop the futile 'self search' and run after His presence with all your might!

He is the very Lover of your soul. He is the One who makes you whole. Love Him, know Him, be His image! This is your first commandment and He is and must be your first love. The secrets of who you truly are are hidden within who He is! God longs to be intimate with you. Don't disappoint Him any longer. Stop for a moment, and fall on your knees. Just worship Him in spirit and truth.

Bring your mind under subjection to your spirit being, and abandon all your personal requests. Just for a few moments, you need nothing from Him but to love Him. He deserves this kind of selfless love and you need to give it to discover your true identity. Don't read another word until you 'love your Lover'.

(Did you stop and love on Him for a few minutes? If so, then keep reading.)

It is so easy to get mixed up in this journey called life. We have a deep longing to love our Father God, and His Son, Jesus Christ who died for us, and yet, we don't really know how to love. It is only by a deep cleansing of flesh nature can we ever imagine or even begin to know how to love without expectations. When we love with expectations that is not love at all, but a very veiled sense of manipulation.

I'm not saying that you should not use your faith and expect heaven to flood your earth days! I am saying that to truly love the Lord with all your heart, mind, and soul, means that I love regardless of anything else. I love simply because I love, not because of what I may gain, or receive in return.

Love is . . . that's all love is. It's ever present; it's ever knowing, and giving, and being. Love has no action.

Please don't misunderstand me here. I am not saying that love does not compel us to action because it certainly does! But the action in itself is not love.

It is the 'compelling action' to love! This is so intricately woven within the DNA of who we are that many times we don't spend the long hours in His presence to decipher the difference. God and His love compels us to love others, and to obey His voice and His commands.

God is love! God does not 'do' love. Therefore, when we are hidden in Christ and our love identity is in tact, we love simply because we long to be with Him; we long to touch Him; we long to LOVE Him!

All other actions that are birthed out of our love for Him is a 'reaction' to love, not love in itself. My love for Him compels me to 'be still' and to 'sit at His feet' and 'be with Him' and 'be in Him.' All of my being is energized, defined, and made whole and perfect IN HIS LOVE FOR ME AS I LEARN TO LOVE HIM COMPLETELY.

When Esther was being prepared to stand before the Persian king, years passed before she was actually presented to him. She was chosen to come inside the kingdom for training. She spent a year in beauty preparations to stand before him and be presented as a potential queen and ultimately a bride for the king.

Once that year was finished then she waited to be called to go in to him. The next year passed and he did not call for her. Then the next year passed and yet, still, he did not call for her. She was now in the fourth year inside the kingdom. One year of preparation and now she was in the third year of waiting to be presented.

Did she just sit around waiting to be presented? I think not. She had full access to the kingdom. She had full access to more preparation and more preparedness. She had the staff and all the eunuchs to learn from of who was the king!

I believe she asked hundreds of questions about who the king was, what did he like, was he like this or like that? How did he like to be addressed? Does he like his queen to do this or that?

I believe she bombarded all of the people who knew him better than she, with so many questions to better prepare her to be presented properly. She was planning on staying, winning, and being accepted. She made preparations for just such an end of this waiting period of her life. She was selfless in her learning, and not selfish! She learned more about him, and in turn, learned more about how to present herself before the king. She pulled on those closest to him to learn more about him.

Why not do the same each day as you pray and spend time with the Lord? Ask the Holy Spirit to teach you how to love the King. Ask the Holy Spirit to teach you how to love! We cannot truly know how to love the Lord, or love one another without being taught by the very Lover of our souls, the one who makes us whole. Why not ask every day, and learn more how to abandon ones' self to fully love Him more?

Now one more time, stop reading for a moment and just love Him. He is love; He deserves for us to learn how to love Him by the Spirit of God. Take the time to write a love song to Him, using only words the Holy Spirit gives you of who He is, of His goodness towards you. I'll leave you space to write it out. Don't judge what you write, or get your head all involved.

Just let your heart pour out to His heart how you truly feel right now about Him. You can write a verse, a chorus, a bridge, two verses, or ten verses but don't hold back and don't fall over in flesh, brain, and mind. Stay in the spirit and write a love song between Lover and lover. Let Him guide you in the words of how to love Him properly.

He is love. He knows how to love. He will show you. Don't be afraid and don't be performing. He is not your judge right now; He is your Lover and Teacher. Let Him show you.

A place for a love song for the Lover of your soul

Chapter Two
Standing Identity

We live in a society that is consumed with how much we can make, what we can achieve, and what we can accomplish and do. We busy ourselves with lists, and goals, and visions, and destinies, and there is nothing wrong with any of that! I am a type A personality and I understand that kind of thinking and have lived almost sixty years in that type of thought process.

I have accomplished much in my lifetime, and by the time I was thirty years old, I had lived 10 lifetimes in comparison to most people. Over the last decade the Holy Spirit has continually challenged me not on my 'doing' but rather on my 'being'. He has driven home to my spirit that much of what we put so much value on, actually does not matter in the realm of eternity, and is misguided at best!

The Spirit of the Lord has spent years retraining me to think more with the value of heaven and not the value of earth. Earth's value system is measured upon what we do. We can't even meet a new person in our lives without the question coming up in the first minute or two of conversation, "So what do you do?" As if that has anything at all to do with who they are, or for that matter who we are!

The Holy Spirit is retraining me to think more in the realm of who I am from the inside out rather than what I do from the outside in. We are a 'works' trained society. We value what we do, but God is training me to value who I am. My being is much more important to the throne room than what I accomplish. Only what we do that is led by the Spirit of God will have any measure of value on judgment day. Even Jesus said while here on earth, " . . . *I do nothing of Myself (of My own accord or on My own authority), but I say [exactly] what My Father has taught Me.*" (John 8:29 AMP)

I have recently been meditating on a verse that I have read hundreds of times and yet never saw one little tiny phrase in it that changes everything for me. It's the story in Luke chapter one about the angel Gabriel and his visitation and conversation with the priest Zacharias.

Gabriel had only been mentioned one other time in scripture and that was almost 600 years prior to his visitation in Luke. He had appeared to Daniel and you can read all about it in that book. He brought Daniel a word from the throne room of heaven, emphasizing that his appearance was in direct response to Daniel's prayers. Then for 600 years we hear nothing from Gabriel.

We find his second visitation to the earth as he brought a word from heaven to Zacharias about the birth of his son, John. Once again Gabriel explained that his visitation was in direct response to prayer. Then we don't hear from Gabriel for another six months when he spoke directly to Mary about her impregnation by the Holy Spirit with Jesus, the Son of God.

In Gabriel's conversation with Zacharias, at one point, Zacharias was kind of disqualifying the word Gabriel brought, and in this disqualification he also disqualified his ability to participate in the miracle and his wife, Elizabeth's, ability to fulfill this word from heaven. It's in verse nineteen that Gabriel made a statement I want you to take a deep look at with me.

Gabriel said, "*I am Gabriel and I stand in the presence of God . . .* "

So Zacharias was having a conversation with an angel who was at least fifteen feet tall, rippling with muscles, filled with the glory and light of God. (I've seen angels and that's what they look like!) In this conversation Zacharias questioned the word that Gabriel brought. Gabriel's response was a resounding statement. I STAND IN THE PRESENCE OF GOD. Ok, but what do you do? I STAND IN THE PRESENCE OF GOD. Yeah, yeah, I got that, but what do you do? I STAND IN THE PRESENCE OF GOD. Talk about an identity settler!

As far as we know, Gabriel only did what the Father told him to do. He was only sent on assignment that we know of through the scriptures in the Bible, three times. Between the first and second assignment was almost 600 years and between the second and third assignment was six months.

What did Gabriel do when he was not on assignment and doing something? He was standing. He was standing in God's presence. His entire eternal mission was to stand in God's presence.

Do you think that we put too much emphasis and value in our lives on the things that we do? Maybe we should be putting more value on how much time we spend standing in God's presence! Let me raise the point that the 'sent assignments' may only happen once we get completely comfortable standing in His presence. Once we are at home in His presence that we never ever want to leave this post, then and only then, are we sent out to fulfill a job or task for the King.

Ephesians 6:13b states in the AMP Bible, " . . . *and having done all [the crisis demands], to stand [firmly in your place].*" Stand! Don't sit around, and don't move; don't run around like a chicken with its head cut off, stand!

All my life I have heard the phrase, "Don't just stand there; do something!" Now I am beginning to believe we should reverse that and say, "Don't just do something, stand there!"

My mama believed that you should not have to be told to do something. She believed that you should be able to see what needs to be done. She would be frustrated with anyone who would just stand around and watch others work while they leaned back, crossed their arms, and just talked to you while you worked!

Having observed that frustration with my mama I learned to pay attention and see what needed to be done and get busy doing it without having to be told! This accentuated my already deep-rooted need to please personality defect, and my great pleasure in doing instead of being still in His presence.

When I saw this great revelation from heaven about Gabriel's biggest job was to simply stand in God's presence, I was moved to tears at my failure of being comfortable in such a position. I cried out to the Lord to teach and train me how to be still and soak in His presence. I asked Him to do what He needed to do to help me overcome my own personality to be whom He created me to be, completely comfortable IN HIS PRESENCE, without an assignment or a job to do.

Stand until you hear from heaven. Stand until you have a word and assignment. Stand, stand, and stand some more. If that is all you ever accomplish on the earth, standing in God's presence puts you in great company!

How do I keep standing in God's presence? I have learned to worship while I wait! The word *wait* in the ancient Hebrew language means *to twist, to twirl, to turn, to intertwine together to make strong.* Waiting God's way is dancing in worship for Him! Worshiping God makes time stand still for me. I can stay in His presence for hours and it seems like minutes if I am truly in pure and holy selfless worship. If my mind is on myself or my needs, or issues, then time seems to stand still and minutes seem like hours. But if my mind is on Him and Him alone, then I am timeless. His infinite presence consumes my finite being and my normal time consciousness becomes time irrelevant!

Having done all the crisis demands, stand firmly in your place. Stand therefore. Stand. Lift your hands to heaven; raise your voice in worship and sing a new song to the King! The clock will stop its incessant 'ticking' when you get lost in His presence. A moment in His presence consumed with Him can feel like hours of pure and cleansing streams from heaven!

He deserves it; you need it! This scripture in Ephesians is in the midst of the plan of putting on the whole armor of God. I have always thought we need armor to fight but in looking closely at this particular passage in its entirety, we need the whole armor of God to stand in His presence.

Once we have on all the pieces of God's armor, we have put on Jesus from head to toe! He is our helmet of salvation to our peace that covers our feet! He is our breastplate of righteousness, which covers our heart and entire region of chest and abdomen area. He is our belt of truth and our shield of faith. He is my sword of the spirit and the ability in the Holy Ghost to pray at all times without ceasing. My armor is actually Jesus and I am hidden within Him. Jesus has done the fighting for us, and the winning too, I might add! It's my job to worship Him in spirit and truth and to know who I am and whose I am!

Once I truly know my identity as a worshiper I am not afraid to stand and worship Him. I don't feel compelled to 'find something to do'! Worshiping God is my warfare! I worship, and He wins! When He wins then I win too, because my entire being is hidden within Him!

This is why I feel so compelled when I am in corporate worship to have the people stand. It is so disrespectful to our God when we are too lazy to stand for a few moments during a service. We stand for the office of the president of the United States no matter what man holds that office. We stand; it's protocol. It's respectful. It's the right thing to do. When a person sits down during worship as if to say, 'Entertain me while I sit here and watch you sing,' I am certain that person has no idea who their God and King is, and who they should be within His presence.

When Esther became queen, chosen by the king, she was given the crown and celebrated as the queen of Persia beside the king. She was within the kingdom as queen for five years before she was challenged to make a stand.

By the time we read of her biggest challenge she had been within the kingdom for nine years. She was chosen and prepared as a potential queen for one year. She waited another three years while the king paraded one girl after another before him night after night. Finally at the end of her fourth year within the walls of the kingdom he called for her.

As she stood before him, he chose her, celebrated her, and put the crown on her head. She then lived inside the kingdom of Persia as his queen for another five years. So by the time we read the words at the end of chapter four and the beginning of chapter five, nine years had passed for Esther.

The law was written and sealed by the king's signet ring that all the Jews, God's chosen people, could be legally killed on a certain day. Mordecai brought word to her, within the walls of the kingdom and the king's palace, of this law.

She had gotten so complacent being protected inside the walls of the king's palace that at first she didn't want to do anything. She tried to disqualify herself and say that the king had not called for her for thirty days.

She tried negotiating with Mordecai that there had to be some other way but there was no other way. She had been given her position for such a time as this. Mordecai challenged her to take her place and use her voice and save the nation of God's chosen people.

She and her maids, along with all of God's people within the Persian kingdom, fasted and prayed for three days, seeking God's will and wisdom. I believe they were also seeking God's anointing for Queen Esther that would be necessary for her to choose to lay down her life to save God's people within the Persian nation.

The fourth chapter ends with the fate filled challenge from Mordecai in Esther 4:14, "*For if you remain completely silent at this time, relief and deliverance will arise for the Jews from another place, but you and your father's house will perish. Yet who knows whether you have come to the kingdom for such a time as this?*"

God will do what He will do. He positions us within the kingdom for certain times in history to use us for His glory and for the saving of nations. We may wait for many years and then all of a sudden the Spirit of God will call us to service of obedience. I've been there, and maybe you have too. Esther most certainly knew that day in the above verse.

She knew she was incapable on her own of fulfilling this call, so she prayed and had everyone else to pray in agreement with her for three days. By the third day, she had the anointing, and had laid down her own life to the point she could obey God. She found her voice and used it to save the nation.

Esther chapter five starts with an astounding few verses that are filled with amazing detail and an eternal shifting of positions for Esther. I believe that Esther and this particular portion of this prophetic book is where we are in history right now. I believe that the bride of Christ is being challenged to find her voice and then ultimately find the courage to use it to save the nation.

I know this is the challenge that I have been faced with since the beginning of the year 2000. I have been working out my own salvation and the call of God on my life for these last days ever since the Lord had me dissect the Book of Esther all those years ago.

I will show you here what you need to see to move to the next place of obedience for God's glory in your own personal life.

Notice in Esther 5:1-3, "*Now it happened on the third day that Esther put on her royal robes and stood in the inner court of the king's palace, across from the king's house, while the king sat on his royal throne in the royal house, facing the entrance of the house. So it was, when the king saw Queen Esther standing in the court, that she found favor in his sight, and the king held out to Esther the golden scepter that was in his hand. Then Esther went near and touched the top of the scepter. And the king said to her, "What do you wish, Queen Esther? What is your request? It shall be given to you-up to half the kingdom!"*"

There is so much revelation in these three verses that I could spend a year here. In fact, back in the year 2000 when I was first receiving this download revelation from heaven, I did spend a year here!

This chapter is about your 'standing identity'. Notice what Esther did after three days of laying her life down at the feet of the Lord in prayer and fasting. She got up on the third day and she dressed herself in her own royal robes. She had these robes for five years but apparently she had never dressed herself, and secondly, I don't believe she had ever 'owned' these royal robes. She had worn them but she had not taken ownership of them, or the authority that came with them!

We are told to wear our robes of righteousness, our robes of salvation, our garments of praise, but do we 'own' these heavenly garments given to us to cover, protect, and position us for our callings? Or do we just borrow them each and every time we go into a service?

Once she put on her own royal robes she stood. For how long we don't know, but we know she didn't grovel, or beg, or bow, or plead with the king not to kill her. She stood in the inner court of the king's palace. She stood. I believe she was 'dead already' so she was not afraid to die. When you are a dead person walking, then death holds no fear for you.

Revelation 12:10-11, "*Then I heard a loud voice saying in heaven, 'Now salvation, and strength, and the kingdom of our God, and the power of His Christ have come, for the accuser of our brethren, who accused them before our God day and night has been cast down. And they overcame him by the blood of the Lamb, and by the word of their testimony, and they did not love their lives to the death.*"

I want you to notice that we overcome and shut up the accuser when we use the blood of the Lamb (covenant), use our own sounds to give testimony of the Lord, and when we are dead already! We don't love our lives; we love our Lord!

I believe this is where Esther was on that fateful day. She had overcome the accuser and disqualifier in her own head, and she was ready to take vows with the king and use her words. She was no longer a silent queen. She had found her voice. And she was not afraid to die, because she realized her silence would kill her, so she might as well die using her voice rather than die in silence!

How about you? Are you willing to die in silence or take the risk and use your voice for the glory of God?

When she stood in her royal robes with a different attitude, a different glow about her, a positional shift had taken place within her heart, which reflected on her face and her body language. She stood. The king noticed.

Yes, he noticed her! How many times have you been in the Lord's presence and yet been so intimidated that you felt you were not even seen? It's time to be seen by the King! Stop being so intimidated and take your place, and stand!

He saw her. He noticed her. He held out his royal golden scepter toward her and she walked toward him unafraid and touched the very top of it.

When the Lord had me take these verses apart in the ancient Hebrew language many years ago, there were some amazing revelations that I had missed for years. First, Queen Esther positioned herself as the queen. The king finally saw her as his queen because she saw herself as his queen.

Next as she stood before him unafraid of dying, he stretched out the golden scepter and she drew near and touched the tip of it. In the ancient language it is a bit more descriptive. It said that as he saw her as his queen, with the stretching out of the golden scepter he actually asked her to marry him and be more than his queen, "Please be my bride, my wife."

By her drawing near and touching the top of the scepter, it was her acceptance of his marriage proposal. As she touched the top of the scepter she answered, "I will marry you. I will be your bride, your wife, your one-partner, and your queen."

We know this to be true by his following statement to her as he offered her *half the kingdom.* When we first read this entire book the king had another queen and in chapter one Queen Vashti was giving a banquet in the palace, which belonged to King Ahasuerus.

Don't miss things when you read the Bible. That one verse in Esther 1:9 is very revealing as to the status of Queen Vashti. She was in the kingdom but owned nothing. The very palace where she was giving her women's banquet did not belong to her. It belonged to the king.

As we read in chapter five the king has offered half his kingdom to Esther. This is a statement of oneness, of being married, not just of fulfilling political positions and titles but a marriage relationship where *all that I have is yours, and all that you have is mine*, type of statement.

Learning to stand in God's presence helps position you for the authority that comes with the title of being a Christian. You have God's authority, God's power, and what He has is yours and what you have is His! Oneness is offered to you, but you must draw near and touch the top of the King of king's scepter to accept your position.

Chapter Three
Bride Identity

Revelation 21:1-11, "Now I saw a new heaven and a new earth, for the first heaven and the first earth had passed away. Also there was no more sea.
Then I, John, saw the holy city, New Jerusalem, coming down out of heaven from God, prepared as a bride adorned for her husband.
And I heard a loud voice from heaven saying, "Behold, the tabernacle of God is with men, and He will dwell with them, and they shall be His people. God Himself will be with them and be their God.
"And God will wipe away every tear from their eyes; there shall be no more death, nor sorrow, nor crying. There shall be no more pain, for the former things have passed away."
Then He who sat on the throne said, "Behold, I make all things new." And He said to me, "Write, for these words are true and faithful."
And He said to me, "It is done! I am the Alpha and the Omega, the Beginning and the End. I will give of the fountain of the water of life freely to him who thirsts.
He who overcomes shall inherit all things, and I will be his God and he shall be My son.
"But the cowardly, unbelieving, abominable, murderers, sexually immoral, sorcerers, idolaters, and all liars shall have their part in the lake which burns with fire and brimstone, which is the second death."
Then one of the seven angels who had the seven bowls filled with the seven last plagues came to me and talked with me, saying, "Come, I will show you the bride, the Lamb's wife."
And he carried me away in the Spirit to a great and high mountain, and showed me the great city, the holy Jerusalem, descending out of heaven from God,
Having the glory of God. Her light was like a most precious stone, like a jasper stone, clear as crystal."

I was only going to give you a couple verses, but when I began to type these scriptures concerning and defining the bride, I just had to put all eleven verses to prove more than one point on who truly is the bride of Christ, the Lamb's wife.

First of all, in our society, we have such mixed views on gender right now. Laws are being written, and social laws are being rewritten of what is acceptable and unacceptable behavior concerning gender. So when I mention gender here, this is not the misused messed up views right now in our social society in which I speak. God made plain that He created two specific genders for all creative species. It is imperative for a species to continue past one generation to have both a male and a female gender.

There is no way for a second generation of a species to be born without both the male and female genders. There must be a life giver and a life receiver. Amazingly, the female gender, in the beginning stage is the life receiver, then turns around and gives birth to the next generation. But don't be fooled. The female does not give life. She gives birth.

It takes the seed of the male to give life. There are no two females or two males mixed together that can give and receive life, and then in turn give birth. It takes both the male and the female gender combined together to produce the creative force of the next generation.

This is how we, as a human race of people, can be the mirror reflection, or very image of God! We must be able to both give and receive life, and then in turn, give birth through the creative ability to produce another generation.

When we study the scriptures concerning husband and wife,

we are told in several different passages that this positioning of male and female as husband and wife on the earth is a natural representation of Jesus Christ as our Bridegroom and the church as His bride.

Why did I bring all this up when dealing with identity? Because we need to face head on the issue of natural human men trying to position and picture themselves as the bride of Christ, just as natural human females have to deal with and position themselves as the sons of God.

So what am I saying then? I am saying that when it comes to the spirit realm, we must readjust our thinking to not be earth bound, or low and slow in human brain levels. We must come up higher and see the bride for who she really is and get passed the gender issue of our socially awkward society. So let's get passed thinking in terms of human sexuality and think in terms of life giving and life receiving, and then birthing terms.

Jesus is the Bridegroom. He is the life giver. No person who is born again would ever try to say that we, as a human race, have any ability to give eternal life. Only Jesus through our born again experience, old things are passed away, all things have become new, can give life! Jesus is the life giver. We are the life receivers when we receive the blood of Jesus, His name, and His authority over sin.

If we confess our sins He is faithful and just to forgive us. We are washed clean by the blood of the Lamb and made whole, and new again. Born again. This is a huge 'do over' for eternity. I get to do eternal life not by my own works or ability but by His work, His plan, His purpose, His blood, His name, His death, resurrection, and ascension.

Revelation 21:1 began with a new ability to see things. John saw a new heaven and a new earth. The first heaven and the first earth had passed away. And just as it seemed an after thought, John said, oh and by the way, there was no more sea. Think about that for a moment. The sea represented in the beginning a separator. The sea separated the dry land from one another. So in the new heaven and the new earth there is no separation at all.

Then John saw a holy city, and he called the city by name, New Jerusalem. This is a brand new city of peace. It's not the old city made over, or made again. It's not the old city restored. It's a new city of peace and it was coming down out of heaven. It was coming down from God! It had been prepared as a bride would be prepared and made ready and adorned for her husband at the altar on their wedding day!

All of a sudden, John heard a loud voice and it was making an announcement. *"Behold, the tabernacle of God is with men, and He will dwell with them, and they shall be His people. God Himself will be with them and be their God. And God will wipe away every tear from their eyes; there shall be no more death, nor sorrow, nor crying. There shall be no more pain, for the former things have passed away."*

Why the big announcement? It's a wedding and a ceremony and there is an end to the old life of the bride and a new life is beginning. So a proclamation had to be sounded. God will be with mankind, His bride, from now on. He will live with His bride, and His bride will be called 'His.' She will not belong to another. She only belongs to Him.

You see why the male gender of humanity must bypass their natural way of thinking to walk in this oneness. It is not about our human way of thinking; this is much higher, much more powerful. This is the highest level ever possible for all eternity of the union between he Lamb and His bride. This is the unity intended from the beginning between God and His creation. The perfect unity finished from the concept of creation until now. And it's here. And we are the receiver of this greatest gift of life!

He wanted to make sure we completely understood the wedding proclamation by adding that God Himself . . . not a substitute, or a stand in, would be with the bride. This is not a rehearsal for things to come later. No! God HIMSELF will be with His bride and He will be her God!

From the concept, understanding, and receiving of this powerful WORD proclamation then the next amazing things will be finished and completed. God will wipe away every tear from every eye! There will never be a need to shed another tear! God will cause there to only be life from that point on, no more death, ever! There will be no more sorrow, ever! There will be no more crying, ever! There will be no more pain, ever! All former things have passed away!

This massive announcement has been made and all have heard, understood and received it! Then God makes the most amazing and awesome statement for all to hear. "*Behold! I make all things new.*"

That's the end of that. Don't ever look back again. Once you have become one with the Bridegroom then never ever dig up your past, never beat yourself up again, never dredge up some old sin, or allow the liar enemy to try and bring up a memory.

It's done. Your Bridegroom has made the announcement. "We are one; we are married. What was yours, I have now received, and covered, and cleansed. There is nothing left of your past. You have no more of your old name, or identity. You are Mine. You have My name, My identity, My blood,

My power, My future, My everything! You are only new, there is no more old."

His vow then states, "*Write, for these words are true and faithful.*" What God has said you can take it to the bank. It is true and it is faithful. He can only be who He is and He is all together true and faithful. His truth and faithfulness have absolved our horribleness. His truth and faithfulness have claimed my old nature and made me new. His truth and faithfulness have overtaken every part of my old being and have dissolved me into nothingness so I have nothing to look back toward. It's all gone! Only He is left within my identity.

He finished His life altering statement with, "*It is done. It is finished.*" Then He proclaims a reminder of who He is. "*I am the Alpha and the Omega.*" In other words, there is nothing but our Bridegroom. Everything is encompassed within the beginning and the end. There is nothing outside of Alpha and Omega, so stop looking!

Then the statement changes to reflect something that we must do. He states that He will give freely of the fountain of the water of life to him who thirsts. Oh, so the Spirit of God, my Bridegroom, is not going to water board me. He is not going to flood me with His presence, power, and purpose unless I am thirsty enough to receive it. If I am not thirsty then no water of life from the fountain of my Bridegroom will be given to me. I must want it! I must hunger and thirst for it!

Lord, I want more of You, more of Your fountain of living water, more of Your presence, power and purpose. Teach us Lord, how to be more hungry and thirsty for You! Until I am hungry and thirsty, I won't have what it takes to overcome. I am an overcomer but I must be hungry and thirsty for it. I want to inherit all things. I want to be His son and I want to call Him my Father!

Did you notice how the voicing changed from that of the bride and Bridegroom to that of the Father and son? That's why in the beginning I mentioned that we must overcome our lower slower way of thinking in terms of bride being feminine and son being masculine. It's all about being what He needs me to be to walk in oneness and unity with Him completely as Bridegroom, Husband, Father, and Spirit!

Then once all of this is settled, you become who you were created to be. It does not happen overnight. This is a lifetime commitment to learn how to get in our rightful place of righteous and holy, positioned at His right hand forever.

All of a sudden, in one verse, the subject seems to change, but not really. Here is a statement of truth for the bride to know and understand. Here are attributes that disqualify her from being His bride. Cowardly, unbelieving, abominable, murderers, sexually immoral, sorcerers, idolaters, and all liars . . . what a list! So a liar and a murderer are on the same list. All those on this list shall have their part in the lake that burns with fire and brimstone, which is the second death. Well ok! That settles that.

Once this list is made and the outcome of being on that list is made clear, then one of the seven angels carrying the seven bowls with the seven plagues came over to John and started talking with him again saying, "*Come, and I will show you the bride, the Lamb's wife.*"

Well, ok. I'm glad to go wherever you say to go as long as you keep that plague in the bowl!

Next thing you know, John is being carried away in the Spirit to a great and high mountain and the angel holding the bowl with the plague in it showed him a great city, the holy Jerusalem, descending out of heaven from God.

This is the second time in these few verses that this specific description is given. So the bride, the Lamb's wife, comes from God and descends out of heaven. She is called the great city, the holy Jerusalem. She has the glory of God and her light was like a most precious stone, like jasper stone, as clear as crystal. A clear jasper stone, as clear as crystal, was the description given by the angel of His bride.

When you continue to read on within the chapter, you will find that the jasper stone is listed as the foundational first stone in verse nineteen. It's also the last stone mentioned in the breastplate of the high priest in Exodus 28:19. Both these positions are very important as we, as the Lamb's wife, are now one with Christ. Since He is the Alpha and Omega, the Beginning and the End, once we are married to Him and one with Him, then we are also represented with both the beginning foundational stone in Revelation and the last stone in Exodus, as the high priest's breastplate covering.

Let's look at one more passage for the bride's identity. Flip back with me in your Bible (you are reading all the scriptures in your own Bible and marking the passages, right?) to the Old Testament.

In Ezekiel 16:1-14, *"Again the word of the Lord came to me, saying,*

"Son of man, cause Jerusalem to know her abominations, and say, 'Thus says the Lord God to Jerusalem; "Your birth and your nativity are from the land of Canaan; your father was an Amorite and your mother a Hittite.

As for your nativity, on the day you were born your navel

cord was not cut, nor were you washed in water to cleanse you; you were not rubbed with salt nor wrapped in swaddling cloths.
No eye pitied you, to do any of these things for you, to have compassion on you; but you were thrown out into the open field, when you yourself were loathed on the day you were born.
And when I passed by you and saw you struggling in your own blood, I said to you in your blood, 'Live!' Yes, I said to you in your blood, 'Live!'
I made you thrive like a plant in the field; and you grew, matured, and became very beautiful. Your breasts were formed, your hair grew, but you were naked and bare.
When I passed by you again and looked upon you, indeed your time was the time of love; so I spread My wing over you and covered your nakedness. Yes, I swore an oath to you and entered into a covenant with you, and you became Mine," says the Lord God.
"Then I washed you in water; yes I thoroughly washed off your blood, and I anointed you with oil.
I clothed you in embroidered cloth and gave you sandals of badger skin; I clothed you with fine linen and covered you with silk.
I adorned you with ornaments, put bracelets on your wrists, and a chain on your neck.
And I put a jewel in your nose, earrings in your ears, and a beautiful crown on your head.
Thus you were adorned with gold and silver, and your clothing was of fine linen, silk, and embroidered cloth. You ate pastry of fine flour, honey, and oil. You were exceedingly beautiful, and succeeded to royalty.
Your fame went out among the nations because of your beauty, for it was perfect through My splendor which I had bestowed on you,' says the Lord God."

I realize this is a long passage and when you read it in its entirety, you will see that it is written to Jerusalem from the prophet Ezekiel prophesying to a people set apart as God's own people. They were not walking with Him as He had designed, and God was using Ezekiel, the prophet, to remind them of the condition in which He found them and how He had cleaned them up as a nation of people, and adorned them, positioned them, as His bride.

The wording and symbolism the Jews understood because of their cultural traditions and could be understood easily through the ornaments, jewelry adornments, and specific fabrics, such as linen, which was always worn by the priests.

If you continue reading after verse fourteen, you will find how displeased God was with them. He had done all to position them to be His bride and yet as a nation of chosen people, they still played the harlot. When our position of our bride identity is set in stone in our hearts, we will not 'play the harlot' and run after other things.

We must *"Seek first the kingdom of God and His righteousness and all these things will be added to you,"* as we are told in Matthew 6:33. When we seek Him and His righteousness first, then the other things we seem to want will be added to our lives. What is so funny, though, is if you truly seek first the kingdom of God AND HIS RIGHTEOUSNESS, many of the things we thought we just had to have, we don't even want!

When our bride identity is in tact, we only have eyes for our Bridegroom. He is all we want. We go through the motions of regular life only to steal a few moments away with Him in His presence. Even if all I have are a few minutes to lift my hands and adore Him, or two minutes in the bathroom stall to give Him glory, I take every moment for Him! He deserves it, and I need it! My bride identity is sealed now.

I have been learning who I am as the bride of Christ for the past sixteen years. It took a huge death in my life to get me to hunger and thirst for Him. Don't follow my example as I had my identity in what I did for Him in His kingdom. Don't get me wrong; I love what I get to do for the King and His kingdom. But that is not my identity any longer. If I never do anything else for my King that humanity would praise or applaud, I know who I am!

My identity is not in my works for my Bridegroom and Father. My identity is in my Bridegroom and my Father! Because of my 'bride' and 'son' identity being settled and sealed, now I get to do so many things for the kingdom of God! Now it is fun and exciting. It's not work, or hard, or tiresome. Why? Because I am doing nothing out of my own strength anymore, but only out of my love for Him. I am sealed and settled in my bride identity.

I have to labor to stay there though. I have to fight my own flesh and self-pride. I have to fight my own natural personality that wants accolades, attention, and approval. I have to fight my own personality to the ground, wrestling the whole time, making sure my spirit man is more fed and stronger than my natural nature.

I have learned and will continue to learn to be in Him first and foremost. As I continue to defeat my old works identity, then my bride identity can come forth more and more each day.

There are so many other scripture passages and stories within the Bible that I could use to help make this bride identity point for you. Esther and Vashti are one and two examples of brides, one who did it right and one who did it wrong. Both had the outcome of their own choices.

I could write an entire book on the amazing love story of Ruth, Boaz, and Naomi. The example of Jesus as our kinsman redeemer, shown through the life of Boaz, then Naomi, as the one who made the wrong choice, and how God used the heathen woman, a Moabite, Ruth, to bring redemption for all.

Ruth chose to follow God and not the god of her homeland, and by this choice, she was personally redeemed, brought redemption for Naomi, and finished the hunger love in Boaz's heart for a bride. Ruth was listed in the genealogy of Jesus giving hope to us all for sinful mankind and a corrupted bloodline to be cleansed and redeemed.

To know who we really are within our Bridegroom, Jesus Christ, is what it all comes down to settling our identity issues. We must stop focusing on who we are not, and focus on who He is! Once we can rein in and harness our self-focus, and turn our attention to the throne of grace, and behold the One who loves us more than we can ever fathom, then and only then can we stop dating our Lord and Savior, and finally marry Him forever!

Will you say "yes" to Him today? If you are already saved, I'm not talking about that. If you are already filled with the Holy Spirit, I am not talking about that. But I will say that you must be born again, and filled with the Spirit of God before you will ever have the strength, power, and ability to say yes to the outstretched scepter in His hand.

Will you draw near and touch the tip of it with the words He longs to hear? **"Yes! I take Your name. I take Your power. I take Your authority. I take all of You and give you all of me. I have no more identity apart from You. I am hidden in Christ and we are one forever.**

Wash me in Your blood, and cleanse me from myself. Rub me with the water of Your word. Anoint me with the oil of Your Spirit. Heal my self-focused heart and teach me how to love You. This is my vow to You, my Beloved, my Bridegroom. I will love You, praise You, worship You, and adore You forever. I will not look at myself another day. I will only gaze on the beauty of You, my Bridegroom from this day forth."

By the power of the Spirit of God within me, I now pronounce you bride and Bridegroom, the Lamb's wife and Kinsman Redeemer. You are one. Walk as one from this day forth.

If you have made this vow, and have received this truth in your heart please sign below.

Bride's signature

____

Jesus already signed His signature with His own blood on the cross. He's been waiting for you for a long time. Welcome home.

Chapter Four
Born to Win Identity

Psalm 139:13-18, "For You formed my inward parts; You covered me in my mother's womb.
I will praise You, for I am fearfully and wonderfully made; marvelous are Your works, and that my soul knows very well.
My frame was not hidden from You, when I was made in secret, and skillfully wrought in the lowest parts of the earth.
Your eyes saw my substance, being yet unformed. And in Your book they all were written, the days fashioned for me, when as yet there were none of them.
How precious also are Your thoughts to me, O God! How great is the sum of them!
If I should count them, they would be more in number than the sand; when I awake, I am still with You."

Many times we see verse fourteen in reference to who we are as winners within the kingdom of God but we need to look at that verse in its context to see the whole meaning of who God has proclaimed us to be! God has spoken us into existence but much more than that! He has spoken who we really are into existence through His word. His word does not change because a human has said something contrary to God's word to you, or about you, etc. His word stands forever.

It's up to us to believe what God has said about us and to us. If we don't believe it, the word does not change, but the outcome for our future days does change. It is up to us to believe what God says about us, and to walk in that 'faith' believing God's power filled word.

You must accept all of what God has said about you personally. God formed your inner parts. Every cell in your body, every sound wave at the core of every cell within your body, God formed and set in motion the frequency of each and every sound wave! God spoke into you and set the rhythm of your cellular system. It is up to you to agree with God's word spoken into you and walk in the fullness of the power of that word filled with God's own sound!

God covered you in your mother's womb. From the tiniest expression of whom you are from within your mother's womb, God Himself covered you. How do we know this? Because His word says that He did. If you can't believe that part of the word of God then you can't believe any part of the word of God.

What do you believe? Do you believe what circumstances, situations, the journey of your life days, what people have said about you and to you? What do you believe? You can choose which path you want to walk by what words you believe!

Can you stretch your faith to believe what God has said, the literal God of the universe, the one and only true God, who created all things? Or you can choose to believe what you have heard all your life, what other lower slower humans have said about or to you, or even the author of all lies who has tried to get you to hear his voice in your ear from the very first day of your life until this very day! What do you choose? Who will you believe?

This is the ultimate life turning point that you must work out for yourself. No one can make this choice for you. No one can help you make it. No one can keep you making the right choice every day for the rest of your life. These are your choices, and yours alone to make and keep on making!

Once you realize that God formed your inward parts and covered you in your mother's womb, then your response to His being with you from conception is to praise Him and make a declaration of whom you really are! You are to declare, **"I am fearfully and wonderfully made!"** Don't stop there; keep making amazing declarations over yourself! Keep saying what God's word says about you.

"I am a work of God and I am absolutely marvelous! Not because I say I am marvelous, but because all of God's works are marvelous and that includes me! And to finish this off and seal it forever, I declare, confess, and proclaim that my soul knows this truth about who I am very well!"

After you have read the above paragraph, please go back and declare the words in bold one more time! You will begin to believe what you say! *"Faith comes by hearing, and hearing by the word of God."* (Romans 10:17) When you say God's word about yourself, then you will begin to have faith in those words that God has already said about you.

This solidifying of your belief system in who God says you are, instead of putting faith in the words that others and the enemy have said, will change the course of your life forever! You will always go where you believe you are going! You will always believe where you are going by what you are saying!

When I was a little girl the milkman, Mr. Horton, confessed over me weekly, "One day, little girl, you are going to be Miss America." I agreed with him and said in my heart, "Yes, that is who I am. I am Miss America." When I finally entered the pageant world at seventeen, I had been confessing and agreeing with the words Mr. Horton spoke over me for twelve years.

I didn't win the first year I entered, or the second, or the third. I lost the local pageants, like Miss Choctaw County and Miss Mississippi State University, year after year. But I didn't change my confession to mirror reflect what I was seeing, hearing, and walking through each time. I continued to say what the prophet, Mr. Horton said. (Yes, the milkman can be a prophet too, if you believe what he said.)

I refused to say what others were saying. I refused to believe what I was seeing, experiencing, and living each day. I said what God said. I am made fearfully and wonderfully. Even in my mother's womb God covered me. I can do all things through Christ who strengthens me. With God all things are possible. Every word from God will be fulfilled.

Was it easy to do this? Absolutely not! It was not easy to continue to believe and confess the word of God when all my situations and circumstances were saying the exact opposite of what God's word said! But one must determine what to believe. Belief and faith are not a finite line that begins at some point and ends when you get the desired result you are confessing and believing.

Faith is. It is ever present and it never ever becomes past. It is not future either. It is . . . faith is ever present and it takes an ever-present relationship with an ever-present Shammah God to continue to stand when others have quit.

Whose report do you believe? We shall believe the report of the Lord! (Isaiah 53:1) So it's not just a question of what you believe but also a question of whom you believe! If the Bible is not true about whom you are, then how can you believe it for any other point as well? You must work out your own salvation and settle this identity of who you are created to be. You were born to win! Hear it, see it, know it, live it!

God's word is filled with so many details that we need to

meditate on to receive all of the depths and dimensions of who we are. In Psalm 139:15,16 the Bible states that your frame was not hidden from God, when you were made in secret, and skillfully wrought in the lowest parts of the earth. God's eyes saw your substance, being yet unformed.

And even more than all of this, you were written in God's book, every day of your life, all the framework of who you are, the very DNA code of your life is all written in God's book! Every day of your life has been fashioned completely and perfectly for you!

All of your victorious identity was sealed and settled by God and even penned by Him in His book before you were more than a thought in God's mind! That is how glorious, and important, and amazing and awesome you are! And that's all before you ever began! That was just the beginning of who you were inside God's creative genius mind!

Are you receiving all of this? Because if you are willing to receive all of this about who you really are, your life can take a massive shift right now, right here, forever. The last two verses are the ultimate icing on the cake, so to speak, for me. *"How precious are Your thoughts to me, O God! How great is the sum of them!"*

God doesn't just have one thought about me! He has so many thoughts about me, and toward me, and to me, and around me, and covering me, if we should try to count them, those thoughts would number more than the sand on the sea shore!

My ultimate response to all this amazing God time He is giving me is such a simple profound statement of who I really am. When I wake each morning, my God is still with me. He never leaves me. He never forsakes me. He loves being with me. He thinks I am awesome.

He waits for me in the secret place. He longs to love me, and be with me. This is who I am, and this is who you are. I know this truth. You must know this truth also to walk in the personal identity of the winner God has hard wired within you.

God knew you. God knows you. This is a word of intimacy. I received this revelation decades ago. The word *intimacy* is simply IN-TO-ME-SEE. To be totally intimate with the Lord, we must allow Him to see in the very depths of who we are.

Why would you hide from Him? He has already seen you, made you, been with you, created you, spoke you into existence, and knows the deepest parts of who you are that even you don't know about yourself! So why hide!

Stop for a moment and just whisper a permission statement to the Lover of your soul, the One who makes you whole. **"Lord, in to me see, right now. I pull back the covers of my heart and ask you to really look inside me. Reveal to me anything and everything that I need to change to be all you created me to be."**

And this prayer above is the last two verses of Psalm 139:23,24, "*Search me, O God, and know my heart; try me, and know my anxieties;*
And see if there is any wicked way in me, and lead me in the way everlasting."

These two verses are the absolute deepest trust levels of intimacy between lovers. Pray this prayer with me aloud. **"Search me, my God. I know You know my heart but**

know me even more. I give You permission to look even closer, even deeper. I give You permission to put me to the test and try me at the very core level of who I am. I won't hide even my deepest insecurities from You. If You see anything in there that is wicked and not like You, show me. Teach me Your ways, how to root out 'self' so that none of that wickedness of pride is left in me. I only want You. IN-TO-ME-SEE. Forever, I will love You. Forever, I will receive Your outpouring love for me."

Now you can walk in who God created you to be. You are born to win. That's your identity. You were created victorious. You don't have to strive or work for what's already coded within your very DNA. Just **BE** who God created you to be even before you were in your mother's womb.

My eventually winning Miss America was a direct result of two things. I kept my confession in agreement with what God's word said about me. I didn't change my confession to reflect what I was looking at over the years.

Once you have a word from heaven and it becomes a part of your belief system, not what you want to believe but in all actuality, what you believe, then you will never change your confession.

If you confess with your mouth and believe in your heart that you are saved, then you are saved! Confession comes first. Even in our daily life, we say things and then we do things. "I am going to the store," then you go to the store. "I am going to bed," then you go to bed. "I am going to read my Bible," then you read your Bible. This is how we live as humans. We say something and then we do it.

When your faith is involved, your confession is the literal

starting line for what has already been finished inside of God's plan for you. That's why we must guard our words so carefully, because many times we change our confession to match or mirror what we are seeing, especially if it takes a while for the plan of heaven to begin to manifest on the earth.

Guard your confession, and make sure you understand that your starting line of all God's plans for you begins with the sound coming forth from your mouth.

I didn't change my confession when I lost the Miss Choctaw County Pageant, or the Miss Mississippi State University Pageant over and over. I just kept saying what God said. "I will win Miss America for His glory."

People thought I was silly, crazy, and a few other not so carefully chosen words. What people thought or said had no bearing on my belief system because I had already settled what God said and had tied my belief system to God's word. Most people never settle that. Until you settle that, other people's words can influence and affect your belief system.

I lost the first year I entered pageants; I lost the second year, and the third year. These losses happened on the local level of the pageant system. I stayed focused and kept my confession in agreement with what God said.

The fourth year I competed, I won my first local pageant as Miss Mississippi State University. A few months later, I competed in Vicksburg, MS, for the crown of Miss Mississippi. I kept my eye on God's finish line, His completed plan for my life. I lost the Miss Mississippi pageant. I came in first runner up, but that's still not winning.

I went back and finished my senior year of college and

completed my degrees. (I received two degrees in four years of college.) I entered another local pageant on the fifth year of competing. My confession had not changed but my prayer had. I stopped praying to win, and I started praying, "Lord, if you can use me more as Miss Starkville than you can as just Cheryl Prewitt, then I want to be Miss Starkville."

I connected my prayer life to a 'garden prayer life' much like Jesus did before the cross. That prayer basically said, "I understand I am at the finish line of Your plan for my life. If the plan has changed, then all I want is Your will, Lord, for my life. Whatever You want, that's what I want."

I didn't change my belief system. I knew the Lord wanted me to be Miss America for His glory. I also knew that pride could infect God's plan if I was not completely humble and submitted at His feet at all times. My will was completely His will. That's all I wanted from that day forth. His will was the ultimate forever plan for me.

I won the Miss Starkville pageant that night and six weeks later I was in Vicksburg, MS, competing (the second time) for the Miss Mississippi title and crown. I won.

Six weeks later I was in Atlantic City, NJ, competing for the Miss America 1980 pageant title and crown. I won. It was September 8, 1979. I was twenty-two years old. It was seventeen years after I had first agreed with God's word through the milkman's prophecy, "One day, little girl, you will be Miss America."

I learned the greatest lesson of all that I continue to walk in to this day. God's plan is absolute and set in stone. His timing is also absolute and set in stone. It is not subject to when I want it, or when I believe it is suppose to happen. God has finished the plan before it ever started.

I must submit my will and my confession to His will. No matter how long in earth's terms it takes to be completed, none of that matters. All that matters is that I know my 'Born to Win Identity' is sealed and settled within my spirit and the plan of God for me.

So, you have a big task to deal with your own mind, will, and emotions. You must bring down old habits of wrong thinking, living, being, and confessing. You must discipline yourself to only say what God says. This bears repeating. You must discipline yourself to only say what God says.

Then, and only then, can you move forward, agreeing with God's plan, His word, His destiny, and His will for your future. You are fearfully and wonderfully made and He knows you! He knows your plan and purpose hidden within the very DNA that is coded within the winner inside you. You were born to win!

Chapter Five
Sound Identity

In Ezekiel 28:12-19, we have an account of who Lucifer was before his fall. We can clearly see that he was an anointed worshiper for the King. He had access where others did not; he walked among the fiery stones. He had nine covering stones all set in gold with pipes and instruments built into the code of his identity. Let's look at the verses that give us such descriptive picture images.

Ezekiel 28:12-19, "Son of man, take up a lamentation for the king of Tyre, and say to him, 'Thus says the Lord God: "You were the seal of perfection, full of wisdom and perfect in beauty.
You were in Eden, the garden of God; every precious stone was your covering; the sardius, topaz, and diamond, beryl, onyx, and jasper, sapphire, turquoise, and emerald with gold. The workmanship of your timbrels and pipes was prepared for you on the day you were created.
You were the anointed cherub who covers; I established you; you were on the holy mountain of God; you walked back and forth in the midst of fiery stones.
You were perfect in your ways from the day you were created, till iniquity was found in you.
By the abundance of your trading you became filled with violence within, and you sinned; therefore I cast you as a profane thing out of the mountain of God; and I destroyed you, o covering cherub, from the midst of the fiery stones.
Your heart was lifted up because of your beauty; you corrupted your wisdom for the sake of your splendor; I cast you to the ground, I laid you before kings that they might gaze at you. You defiled your sanctuaries by the multitude of your iniquities; by the iniquity of your trading; therefore I brought fire from your midst; it devoured you, and I turned

shes upon the earth in the sight of all who saw you. All who knew you among the peoples are astonished at you; you have become a horror, and shall be no more forever.'"

When you count the stones that Lucifer had as his covering stones, there were nine in all. When you compare those nine stones to the high priest's breastplate covering, you will find these same nine stones plus three more in addition to them. You can find the same twelve stones listed in Revelation 21:19 as the foundations of the city of the New Jerusalem, the bride, the Lamb's wife.

The bottom line is Lucifer was anointed, and ordained, and given the nine covering stones set in gold with pipes and timbrels within his workmanship. He had instruments inside of his being, and his outer covering was beautifully magnificent. He had access to the mountain of God and he was anointed to cover that mountain of worship.

He walked back and forth in the midst of fiery stones on the mountain of God. He was perfect! God said that Lucifer was perfect from the day he was created! And then he wasn't perfect any more.

Many musicians and singers, who want to be worshipers, seem perfect to pastors when they bring them on their staff and give them much face to face time with the people in the church. They seem perfect, and honestly, much like Lucifer, they probably were perfect when they first came.

This is what we must fight against and protect from as gifted and talented musicians who are called to be worshipers. I call it the Luciferian spirit. This spirit tries to get a person, who is perfect in their calling, to fall prey to the spirit of pride, just as the first lead anointed worshiper fell.

God said Lucifer was perfect, until . . . we must guard our hearts against the 'until moments' that can get us off course of our calling and anointing.

If Lucifer would have constantly reminded himself that his anointing and calling was for the great I AM who had created him, then maybe he could have avoided the 'until moment'. But he allowed his heart to get lifted up because of his beauty, and he corrupted his wisdom for the sake of his own glory. He became filled with violence and it caused him to sin.

Who was once perfect from the day he was created became profane, corrupted, defiled, devoured, turned to ashes in the sight of all who saw him, and cast out of God's presence and away from his founding created purpose. All who knew Lucifer among the peoples were astonished at him, and he became a horror and quickly came to an end with God's pronouncement of "Lucifer shall be no more forever!"

I go into much depth of this entire revelation in my book *Tones of the Throne Room.* The revelation is powerful and life changing once we realize that we have the power within our choice to stay clean, holy, and perfect for God's use as His instruments of righteousness. It's my choice and it's your choice too.

What I want you to realize is your identity as a worshiper is strongly connected to the sounds within you that you allow to become the sounds that come out of you. When Lucifer was walking in his purpose, his sounds of worship reflected what was designed from within him. Once he changed his tone, once he changed his sound to reflect a spirit of pride instead of a spirit of pure and holy worship, he became corrupted. His own sound brought about his demise from within his very being.

That is why we must protect the sounds we allow to come forth from our being. Out of the abundance of the heart the mouth (makes sound) speaks! Your mouth is always sounding what is in your heart.

When you are a called and anointed worshiper, your primary focus is to protect your heart from being led astray to 'self focus.' What about me? When do I get my reward? When does God meet my needs? When will He answer my prayers? And so on and so forth . . . self focus.

You were created to worship the King of kings! Your sound is His sound. He promised you He will take care of you, but when you corrupt your own future by the thoughts you allow to become rooted in your heart, you have sealed your future with a fall!

Lucifer didn't start corrupted. He became corrupted. Somewhere along the line of his daily walking back and forth in the midst of the fiery stones of God's holy mountain with amazing close access to God's throne and God's presence, he became self focused and it brought about massive internal corruption. He went from *perfect* to *cast out* with one 'until moment'.

In Matthew 16:19, Jesus made a powerful statement for worshipers to grasp about their sounds, tones, and frequencies.

"*And I will give you the keys of the kingdom of heaven, and whatever you bind on earth will be bound in heaven, and whatever you loose on earth will be loosed in heaven.*"

Notice the prepositional phrase 'keys of the kingdom'. This is the most powerful phrase that I have ever found in the Bible concerning worship.

If I asked you for the key to your car or the key to your home, I would use the preposition 'to'. But the phrase Jesus spoke used a different preposition. He used 'of' instead of 'to.' All my life when I read this verse I had the mental picture of a massive key that unlocked the door to the kingdom of heaven. I had one key in my mind's eye. But the scripture uses the plural of the word 'keys'.

Jesus said 'keys of the kingdom'. He changed the entire meaning by making *keys* plural and by using the preposition 'of'. The kingdom of God is singular. There is only one kingdom of heaven, therefore if it were a *key* to the kingdom, then there would only be *one key* to *one kingdom*. But this is not a reference to a key to a kingdom. This is a reference to multiples keys of a kingdom.

From my music background, I now realize I should have seen this much sooner than I did, but honestly, in my wisdom years, I understand that we don't see any revelation until the Spirit of God opens our eyes to see and hear what the Spirit is saying through His word!

Music is a language, and it has its own language rules and standards. The main language of music is written with the seven keys everyone knows as 'Do-Re-Mi-FA-Sol-La-Ti'. These seven different tones in our musical scale make up a full circle of tone. When the first tone is repeated to complete the circle of eight tones, we call this an octave or a full scale. Eight tones make an octave and we sing it as 'Do-Re-Mi-Fa-Sol-La-Ti-Do'.

These are not just tones, or sounds. They are frequencies assigned to each tone within a given scale. As the octaves rise higher and higher in pitch, the frequencies get faster and faster. If the scale is descending rather than ascending then the frequencies get slower and slower, which causes the tones to go lower and lower in sound waves.

If you are not a musician, you may already be 'lost in translation,' but don't give up. You will grasp enough for the revelation to be revealed to you if you ask the Spirit of God to show you what you can't see with your natural mind. All revelation is given from above so know that God wants you to see and understand this so you can control your own tongue and sound can only come forth out of your instrument from heaven!

When Jesus said, *"I will give you the keys of the kingdom,"* I believe He was referring to the musical keys we call the 'Do-Re-Mi-Fa-Sol-La-Ti'. These seven tones create a full circle of sound and frequency. Each one is designated as a key.

When we assign the different intervals of sound to a specific key on an instrument, then we begin to easily see why Jesus would use the words 'keys of' instead of 'key to'. In music a particular key of frequency is assigned an identifying letter.

In the music language, there are only seven different lettered keys as well. For example, in our English language, we have 26 letters of the alphabet, A through Z. In the music language, there are only seven different letters, A through G. Once you get to G, the next letter begins again with A. It is called a circle in music ever spiraling higher or lower depending on your direction. On a piano, there are seven octaves and a third that complete a full keyboard. This is a range of 88 keys. (This includes the half tones as well as the whole tones!)

I believe when Jesus said that He would give us the keys of the kingdom, He was referring to our sounds, our tones, our own frequencies within our ability to make sound. I believe Jesus was saying that through our own sound waves coming forth from our human instruments we can bind on earth and loose on earth what will have been bound or loosed already in heaven.

Our sound actually brings what is eternal to our natural realm. Our sound can bring heaven to earth for us. Our sound can cause those things that are not to BE! Our sound wave is a key of the kingdom that causes things to be loosed that should be loosed and bound that should be bound!

By using the keys of the kingdom that Jesus has given us, we can walk this earth knowing who we are and the power that we have while here on earth. Once we realize we have these keys and sounds within us, we can understand more fully the scripture in Proverbs 18:21, *"Death and life are in the power of the tongue . . ."*

We hold the sounds within our cellular level to change the course of death or life! We can speak with the power of our tongues and bring dead to life, or life to death! What are you saying that you should not be saying? What should you be saying that you have not been saying? Get your sound identity in place and start using it to bring heaven to earth, and the will of the Father to the realm of the earth!

Jesus gave us seven keys of the kingdom. Of course there are seven because that is the 'it is finished' number and that totally coincides with the musical language of a completed circle of sounds in seven tones (Do-Re-Mi-Fa-Sol-La-Ti). These seven keys are different frequencies that bind and loose the realm of heaven to the earth!

When Lucifer fell from his position on the mountain of God as anointed worshiper, he lost his covering stones. Stones have frequency and they make sound! There are entire fields of rocks discovered now in Bucks County, PA, where the rocks are all singing! Each rock has a unique and distinct musical tone or sound when struck. The fields are singing! The rocks are crying out!

Lucifer lost his covering stones and in those stones were his sounds, his frequencies, and his worship. We have a seven-toned musical scaled language that is universal for all. Music has no language barrier between nations and tongues. It is understood by the entire world.

So if the musical language of seven toned scales are the sounds within the realm of heaven that Jesus has given to us to use to bind and loose, to create life or death, then where are the other two sounds? Lucifer had nine covering stones, and the music language only has seven tones.

Let's take a look at Revelation 1:18. Jesus has given us the keys of the kingdom of heaven. We have received those in sound waves and tones that come forth from our instrument of righteousness when we use our sounds to worship the King! So where are the last two stones and their frequencies of sound?

Once again, Jesus gave us the answer to everything within His word. Revelation 1:18, reveals the last two sounds and Jesus has them now!

"I am He who lives, and was dead, and behold, I am alive forevermore. Amen. And I have the keys of Hades and of Death."

Once again, Jesus has keys. He has two more keys, #8 and #9 stones with frequency. When Lucifer fell, he lost 7 of his covering stoned frequencies, but he kept the last two sounds of hell and death. This explains how Lucifer, now Satan, could go before God when the 'sons of God' were called to present themselves before the Lord.

Job 2:1, "Again there was a day when the sons of God came to present themselves before the Lord, and Satan came also among them to present himself before the Lord."

As long as Satan had the ability to make sound, he could present himself along with the others before the Lord. I believe Jesus had enough of this and longed to silence the enemy once and for all. I believe part of the plan of the cross was to silence the accuser of the brethren forever.

The work of the cross was finished when Jesus breathed His last breath and said, *"It is finished."* The veil was torn from top to bottom giving access to all who will believe behind the curtain that once separated God's presence from humanity. The beginning of rebuilding the ruins of worship began on the cross with the tearing of the veil.

When we become the kings and priests that we have been DNA coded to be, then our purpose is secure, and we can stand in the gap between the very presence of Almighty God and mankind hidden inside of Jesus Christ.

But Jesus didn't just stop with His sacrifice of Himself as the eternal and forever Passover Lamb of God. Once He finished His earth journey, the scripture makes it clear that Jesus then went to hell and while He was there He did a final work for us. He took back the last two sounds that Satan had, and Jesus silenced Satan forever! He took back the last two frequencies, the last two sounds, the sounds of death and hell!

Jesus has silenced the accuser of the brethren and denied him access before the throne of God forever. Look at Revelation 12:10-11 and read it with understanding of past, present, and future verb use.

"Then I heard a loud voice saying in heaven, 'Now salvation, and strength, and the kingdom of our God, and the power of His Christ has come, for the accuser of our brethren, who accused them before our God day and night, has been cast down.'
"And they overcame him by the blood of the Lamb and by the word of their testimony, and they did not love their lives to the death."

Many interpret this to be happening in the time frame of the seven years of tribulation, but I believe for those of us who have eyes to see, and ears to hear, we can see the truth for us now! Jesus silenced Satan and took back the last two sounds he had kept after his great fall. Satan had used those sounds to have entrance before the Lord. When he went before the Lord, he used the sounds of death and hell to accuse us, the brethren, day and night.

The final statement in that verse is a past tense verb. The accuser of the brethren has been cast down! He has been cast down because of what Jesus did after the cross by going into the depths of hell and taking the last two sounds Satan had. The only way Satan can ever make another sound is when he plays a human instrument!

Unless humanity allows Satan to use their voices to make a sound, he has been silenced! Humanity still has a free will and freedom to choose. Many humans still choose to use their sounds for death and hell, instead of life and heaven!

Who is playing you? What sounds are you making? You are an instrument, created to be played by the Spirit of God on this earth! But you have free will, and you can make the sounds of Satan as well, if you give him permission to play your instrument.

Romans 6:13, "And do not present your members as instruments of unrighteousness to sin, but present yourselves to God as being alive from the dead, and your members as instruments of righteousness to God."

There are many people who call themselves Christians, but they are most definitely instruments of unrighteousness. The enemy is using their vocal cords.

Their tongue is a perfect example of James 3:6, *"And the tongue is a fire, a world of iniquity. The tongue is so set among our members that it defiles the whole body, and sets on fire the course of nature; and it is set on fire by hell."*

We are tuned for heaven and the sounds of eternity, but we still have free will, and when we allow the enemy to play us by manipulating our thinking and our emotions, we can easily have an out of control tongue that sets nature on its course instead of setting God on His course!

Make a choice today to be an instrument of righteousness! Don't allow Satan who was silenced on the cross by Jesus when Jesus took back the last two sounds, the last two 'keys of hell and death,' to play you as an instrument of unrighteousness. Now Jesus has all nine keys!

He has the keys of the kingdom and he has obtained, and still has now, the last two keys of hell and death. Don't let the enemy play your instrument for his glory when you were created and tuned before you were in your mother's womb to make the sounds of heaven!

God loves the sound of righteousness! Hebrews 1:9 shows us such an awesome promise when we protect our sound to keep it holy and righteous! The Bible states, "*You have loved righteousness and hated lawlessness; Therefore God, Your God, has anointed You with the oil of gladness more than Your companions.*"

This verse is a quote from Isaiah 61:1, 3, which is a prophetic word for Jesus, and since we are hidden inside Christ, then the words that have been prophesied for Him also apply to us! When we hate lawlessness and love righteousness, God anoints us with the oil of gladness more than those among whom we are associated!

I want to have my sound identity in such an awesome place of righteousness that the oil of gladness keeps me covered and heavily anointed at all times! You can claim this same promise as you walk in the perfect will of the Father as you seek after His righteousness and His will every moment of every day. Protect your sound identity and never allow anyone else to say who you are! You say who you are inside of Christ!

Chapter Six
Crucified Identity

Who are you really? You are not identified with what you have gone through or what has happened to you throughout your life. Oh, you may be saying, "Oh, yes I am!" This has happened to me and that has happened to me and it has helped shape the way I think and react. That may be true, but it has no right to your identity. It only has affected you because you have allowed it to do so.

What has happened to me in my life has no right to my identity. I am not a victim. I don't wear what I have been through like a badge of honor. Those things that have tried to break me through the journey of my life have no part of my identity. I am not a cancer victim just because I have overcome cancer three times. I don't wear that as a badge.

I am not a cripple, or scarred, simply because I walked with a limp for six years of my teenage life, or because I have had over 150 stitches on my face. I am not a sum of the horrible things that have happened to me.

My identity is not in what has happened to me over the years, but rather my identity is settled and sealed within the blood and name of Jesus Christ. It's my choice whether I allow myself to become a victim or whether I live victoriously.

Galatians 2:20 states, "*I have been crucified with Christ; it is no longer I who live, but Christ lives in me; and the life which I now live in the flesh I live by faith in the Son of God, who loved me and gave Himself for me.*"

When I truly realize what the scripture above is offering me, I can walk in total victory at all times and not allow the earthly flesh journey to become a part of my identity.

People can say horrible things to us. We say horrible things about us too. We stand in front of the mirror and criticize God's image, and many times we rehearse what others have said about us as if it were truth. Even a lie will operate as truth in your life IF you believe the lie. Don't believe lies about who you really are. Only believe what God has said about you!

If you are 'dead' to yourself, then nothing anyone says, whether praise or criticism, can get you off track of the path God has ordered for you. I have been working on, 'being a dead woman walking,' for many years.

It's a daily dying process. Paul said it very clearly in 1 Corinthians 15:31, "*I die daily.*" That was a huge revelation when you realize that, no matter how deep in the presence of God you may go today, after you get a little sleep, your flesh is refreshed and back alive again, and you have to die to self all over again!

Paul said in Romans 8:4-14, "*That the righteous requirement of the law might be fulfilled in us who do not walk according to the flesh but according to the Spirit,*
For those who live according to the flesh set their minds on the things of the flesh, but those who live according to the Spirit, the things of the Spirit.
For to be carnally minded is death, but to be spiritually minded is life and peace.
Because the carnal mind is enmity against God, for it is not subject to the law of God, nor indeed can be.
So then, those who are in the flesh cannot please God.
But you are not in the flesh but in the Spirit, if indeed the Spirit of God dwells in you. Now if anyone does not have the Spirit of Christ, he is not His.
And if Christ is in you, the body is dead because of sin, but the Spirit is life because of righteousness.

But if the Spirit of Him who raised Jesus from the dead dwells in you, He who raised Christ from the dead will also give life to your mortal bodies through His Spirit who dwells in you.
Therefore, brethren, we are debtors, not to the flesh to live according to the flesh.
For if you live according to the flesh you will die; but if by the Spirit you put to death the deeds of the body, you will live.
For as many as are led by the Spirit of God, these are sons of God."

There are many scriptures that prove this point, that we are to live dead to flesh and alive to the Spirit of God. It's obviously possible or there would not be so many scriptures supporting this premise. There are many people who say they love God. There are many people who say they are called according to His purpose, who say they are worshipers of the most-high God, and yet they live in the flesh, they walk after the flesh, and they fulfill the lusts of the flesh!

This ought not to be! We are to die daily to our flesh and this takes much effort of being in His presence, and feeding our spirits, and starving our flesh!

One day I was meditating on this and trying to figure out how to live in this world without sin in my daily life. I had spent much time in the books of 1st, 2nd, and 3rd John, and if you read these three little books, there are some very poignant verses to support we can live without the constant agony of sin in our lives.
He speaks to me through His word, first and foremost. He speaks to me when I am alone with Him in the secret place, heart to heart. He speaks to me through dreams occasionally, and He speaks to me through visions.

To be unoffendable, I must stay dead in the flesh and alive in the Spirit of God at all times. People will always say things that can get you distracted from your task at hand. You must pray daily for the Lord to give you 'ears to hear what the Spirit is saying.'

Sometimes people say appraising comments and tell us things that get us to thinking that we are awesome. Sometimes people say offending things that cause us to think negatively about ourselves. Regardless of what is said to you, those words can get you off your God assignment. As long as people's words can influence you, you are still in the dying process, and you must be aware that YOU ARE NOT DEAD YET.

If criticism can get you off, then so can applause. We must not be moved one way or the other by what people say. Dead people are not moved by the words of others. Dead people are walking so deeply in the love of God, that they hardly notice when done wrong. Dead people are walking in love.

1 Corinthians 13:4-8 sums it up best for me, "*Love suffers long and is kind; love does not envy; love does not parade itself, is not puffed up; does not behave rudely, does not seek its own, is not provoked, thinks no evil; does not rejoice in iniquity, but rejoices in the truth; bears all things, believes all things, hopes all things, endures all things. Love never fails.*"

To walk in the above statements is a fulltime lifelong mission. I must sheriff my own life, heart, mind, and mouth if I am to walk in the love that has been afforded me through the blood of Jesus Christ. My identity is His identity, and His identity is all encompassing love. I long to know Him and be like Him in His amazing love!

To walk with Christ means to be separate from others when necessary. 2 Corinthians 6:17-18 , *"Therefore, 'Come out from among them and be separate,' says the Lord. 'Do not touch what is unclean, and I will receive you. I will be a Father to you, and you shall be My sons and daughters, says the Lord Almighty.'"*

I separate myself from others who are not clean. I separate myself from those who say one thing but their lives reflect another. I separate myself from unholy, unrighteous, unfruitful lives, even if they call themselves Christians. I can examine and judge the fruit of their mouths and the fruit of their actions.

I separate myself to live a holy, righteous, and clean life before the Lord. I will not touch or hang with unclean, and the Lord will receive me because of my choices to be an instrument of righteousness for His glory.

He will be my Father. He calls Himself Father when He thinks of me. I will be His daughter and you can be too. You can be His son. He will call me daughter. He will call you son and daughter too. This is what the Lord Almighty says; I believe Him. I agree with Him.

My identity is sealed and settled inside of Christ. I AM A WORSHIPER OF THE MOST-HIGH GOD. That is what I do, but most of all, that is who I AM! I am crucified with Christ! It is no longer I who lives, but Christ who lives in me!

Chapter Seven
Victorious Identity

Your belief system can greatly affect your worship. If you know who you are in Christ, then what others have said, what you have walked through, the pain and scars of your past will have no affect on your worship. Only your God identity has a right to who you are as you stand in the throne room of heaven and worship the King forever and ever!

I grew up in Choctaw County, MS. Notice I didn't even name a city or town, because I grew up out in the country of the county! I grew up on a dirt road on a farm. I was in a car wreck when I was eleven years old, crushing my left leg, fracturing my back, and had hundreds of stitches on my face that left many scars.

I determined that I would not be a product of my environment. I determined that I would not be a sum of tragedies that have riddled my life. When my classmates called me a cripple, I would loudly declare, "I am a miracle."

Doctors had said that I might never walk again, but after three months in a body cast the Lord put a bone in my left leg that wrapped all the fragmented pulverized pieces of shattered bone until there was a new bone that covered all the other pieces. I knew that I was a miracle, and what others said from their observation could not shake my belief system of what I knew to be true.

You see, when you truly believe something, then the words, judgments, opinions of others, even those who are well meaning, cannot shake what you already know to be true. That's your belief system.

I had lived through a miraculous encounter with the Lord,

and no one could take that experience from me by his or her negative beliefs. I knew that I knew that I knew what had happened to me. Deep down in my 'knower' I knew that I was changed forever. Of that I was certain.

As I mentioned in chapter four, Mr. Horton, the milkman, had a very strong influence over my belief system. His words changed the course of my life by changing how I saw and spoke about myself. When I was five years old, we had just opened a little country store out in the country, and every Tuesday, Mr. Horton brought the milk and other dairy products in his big truck for us to sell that week. The moment he pulled up between the house and the gas pumps, I would jump out the front door, banging the screen door as I ran. He would get out of his truck, and come around to the back where the big door was, open it, and climb inside the refrigerated truck. I was right behind him.

Even though I was small, I would manage to climb up the back bumper, and into the truck right behind Mr. Horton. He was happy, and jovial, and kind of round like Santa Claus, and I loved when he came each week.

I followed him around; every step he made I was right behind him! Each and every Tuesday he would tell me the same thing. "One day, little girl, you are going to be Miss America." I would smile and nod my head, and agree with him every Tuesday!

His words affected my belief system within me. His words gave me hope and a future and, yes, even a plan from God. His words spoke of future and were not affected by poor, country dirt road, flour sack dresses, eventually, crippled and scarred. His words were life, and future, and hope, and healing! Yes! I would agree with those words for the next seventeen years until they were fulfilled.

You see, you decide what you believe about yourself and your future. You must decide what you truly believe. I earned Miss America and that crown through years of believing in who I am for God's glory, through years of being called a cripple, and scarred, and many other things that were said about me. I only believed the good things. That's all I would agree with in my heart.

At seventeen years old, I entered my first pageant, and you can read about the next five-year journey in great detail in my first book, *A Bright Shining Place*. In the pageant world, I lost the first year, and the second, and the third. I finally won a local pageant the fourth year, only to go to the Miss Mississippi Pageant and come in first runner up, which is not winning! I went back the fifth year, entered and won a local pageant, went on to the Miss Mississippi pageant and won also. Then by September 8, 1979, I became Miss America 1980 for the glory of God!

This all happened because of my belief system. What do you believe about yourself? You become what you believe about yourself and your future. I earned the crown of Miss America 1980 through years of competitions, years of preparation, discipline, endurance, and an attitude that was honed to believe in the future and never look back at the past. I would not quit, I would not give up, and I would not allow the words of others to shape and set my destiny.

I would not allow the words of the enemy to create an earth bound, fear filled, defeated identity that was not God's plan for my life. With that crown came the authority of a good job for a year, a title of "Cheryl Prewitt, Miss America 1980" for a lifetime, and the authority to pray for this nation and stand in the gap in the throne room of God for America for all eternity.

The "Miss America" title was backed by the power of the *Miss America Organization.* The power of that organization had been established in 1921 and had stood undaunted. During my year I used it for God's glory. I gave my testimony every day, and many days a dozen times! I shared, prayed, and led people to Jesus Christ.

I laid hands on the sick in shopping malls, local, and state pageants, and churches. I used that year, every day of it, for God's glory. My life had been set in motion for such a time as this, and I was not going to waste one minute of it.

To say the leadership of the Miss America pageant was not pleased with me was an understatement. You see, I believed then, and I still believe this today, that for one year, Miss America became whoever had the title. They believed that the person who won became Miss America. But Miss America, in itself, has no identity.

I discovered this a few months into the year and began to work hard to not lose myself within the daily routine of fulfilling the role. So instead of believing that I had become Miss America, I knew that for one year, Miss America became me, Cheryl Prewitt. That's how I lived every day and kept my identity as a Christian and God's woman in tact. It was not easy walking out the destiny of God's plan when everyone around you believed something else. But it is possible. All things are possible to those who love God and are called according to His purpose!

When I finished my year and the next Miss America was crowned, I asked the leadership where should I stand after I placed the crown on the head of the new Miss America. With disdain, and almost hatred in his voice, he simply said,

"You can get off the stage. We have had enough of Jesus for a lifetime."

Wow! Shocking and hurtful words came hurling at me with such vehemence! At first my heart was hurt, as I knew I had been an excellent Miss America, both for the organization, and most definitely, as a representative of Jesus Christ.

I stepped away, but not without realizing that when you walk in your calling and fulfill your own God given destiny, others may not understand what you are doing, or who you truly are. As I began to realize the power of those words spoken to me, and words spoken into the heavenlies, I begged the powerful man not to make such a statement against the pageant in the kingdom of God.

He laughed at me, but I knew the fate of the pageant, and the influence it had once held was in jeopardy and quite possibly sealed as 'Ichabod' (The glory of God had gone) from the moment those words were spoken. Now almost forty years later, we can see the digression of the once very powerful system to almost non-existent and most definitely not the influential position it was during my year and former years.

The power of the Miss America pageant has been lost, and the identity of it has been shattered. I believe all because of the words of leadership spoken against Jesus Christ, the King, on that fate filled day.

I worked hard during those twelve months to hold on to my God identity and use the name that had been given to me. When people would call me Miss America, I would say, "My title is Miss America. My name is Cheryl Prewitt, please use my name."

Of course, I was honored to be Miss America 1980, but in

conjunction with my name. I realized that at the end of twelve months someone else would have the crown and the title and I could not afford to lose my identity even for one year.

You cannot afford to lose your God identity. You must work to keep it in the forefront of your belief system. You must know who you are and whose you are. When I became Miss America 1980, there was a shift in the heavenlies.

I fought to keep my identity during those months while I wore that crown. I knew the year could swallow up my God given destiny and identity, and it was up to me to fight to remember whom I am. Do not allow the journey you are currently on to swallow up your destiny and identity that God has created inside of you.

I won the Miss America 1980 title for His glory. I won to fulfill His will, not my own. He sent the milkman, Mr. Horton, to prophesy to me when I was a little girl, and give me a word that I could hold on to as I journeyed through years of being crippled and scarred. Many have asked me if Mr. Horton knew that I had won Miss America. Sadly, he died a few months before my crowning, but I think he knew as he cheered me on from heaven while hearing, “Well done, thy good and faithful servant. Welcome home.”

You are not a sum of all the bad things, or even the good things, that have happened to you. You are fearfully and wonderfully made, and God’s plan was set in motion for you even before you were in your mother’s womb.

I have refused to be identified by and with my journey. Our daughter died of a brain tumor. I determined that grief would not become my identity. I have had cancer three times and a heart attack, and many other things have happened to my body, but none of them are my identity. I am not a cancer survivor. I am a cancer overcomer through the blood and name of Jesus! Life is filled with many difficulties, but those difficulties have no right to become your identity.

No matter what people have said about or to you; no matter how many times you have been told you can't, or you don't have the ability, or you don't have the talent, or you won't amount to anything, or you are a loser, or whatever stupid words have been said to you, or about you; none of those words have any right to affect who you really are!

God programmed your DNA with His sound, His destiny, His plan and purpose. What does God say about you? That is what you should be saying about yourself, too! Agree with what God says, and your victorious identity will be sealed and settled in your heart and belief system too! Say what God says about you out loud every day!

You are victorious.
You are a winner.
You are an overcomer.
You are powerful and power filled through Jesus Christ.
You can do anything in the name of Jesus.
You can become anything and everything you were created to be.
You have the same rights as Jesus Christ because He is your Savior and Lord.
You can do all things through Christ who strengthens you.
Greater things than Jesus did, while here on this earth, you are capable of doing while you are here on this earth!
You can go through the storms of life.
You can walk through the fire and not smell of smoke.
You can walk on the unstable waters of calamity and keep on walking!

You are created to live, and breathe, and have your being inside Christ.
Your words are powerful and creative.
You are victorious; you can do anything!

That's what I say about you. Now you say it about you too!

I am victorious.
I am a winner.
I am an overcomer.
I am powerful and power filled through Jesus Christ.
I can do anything in the name of Jesus.
I can become anything and everything I was created to be.
I have the same rights as Jesus Christ because He is my Savior and Lord.
I can do all things through Christ who strengthens me.
Greater things than Jesus did, while here on this earth, am I capable of doing while I am here on this earth!
I can go through the storms of life.
I can walk through the fire and not smell of smoke.
I can walk on the unstable waters of calamity and keep on walking!
I am created to live, and breathe, and have my being inside Christ!
My words are powerful and creative.
I am victorious; I can do anything!

Say this until you believe it! Write it out and post it on your mirror, in your car, and on your refrigerator door! Don't forget who you are! You are victorious!

Chapter Eight
Divine Government Identity

Hebrews 12:22-24, "*But you have come to Mount Zion and to the city of the living God, the heavenly Jerusalem, to an innumerable company of angels, to the general assembly and church of the first born who are registered in heaven, to God the Judge of all, to the spirits of just men made perfect, to Jesus the Mediator of the new covenant, and to the blood of sprinkling that speaks better things than that of Abel.*"

The earthly manifestation of Mount Zion was established during the reign of King David, as a place where perpetual worship was offered. There twenty-four hours a day, seven days a week, worship went forth for the King of Kings! The worshipers faced the altar of the Holy of Holies with their backs to the inner court where people were, and they became invisible worshipers.

What made them invisible? Their identifying features, their faces, were turned toward God! This caused the worshiper to only receive identity from the One they were facing . . . God! In God's presence you can discover your true identity.

They were not performing for the people in the inner court. They were worshiping the King in His holy place! To the people they had no identity at all, as only the back of their heads could be seen. This is how it should always be in worship. People should not be allowed to applaud the personality, or ability, or talent of one who is called a worshiper. We applaud the King and His presence!

Worship is strictly for the One being worshiped, not for the entertainment of people. The first order of business for King David was to put God on the throne in worship and remove the veil and replace it with worshipers facing His presence.

The worshipers were cleansed and made ready as priests to worship God in spirit and in truth. He literally turned the worshipers around so not one gifted person could receive any glory, but only the one true God could receive all the glory!

People think that Zion is about worship. But Zion was never intended to be about worship. Zion was intended to be about the purpose of worship. There is a huge difference between 'worship' and the 'purpose of worship!' One of the reasons our nation and its government are in the mess that it is in right now is because we, as God's people, don't understand or implement the purpose of worship for which it was intended.

Worship has a purpose, but how can we fulfill the purpose of worship if we have no idea that it has one? Worship is not a warm up for the sermon or a time frame allotted to give the people enough time to get their children to children's church and get in their seats! Worship has a divine ordered purpose. King David commissioned worship to cultivate and host the presence of God, so that from God's presence, he, as king, could govern the nation. This is the purpose of worship. Out of proper, true, and pure purposeful worship is to flow the governing authority of God through His church, and, ultimately, through His nation.

We will never turn a nation back to God until we turn the church of that nation back to God! We cry out, "America is one nation under God," but there is absolutely no evidence of that left within the government of this land. The laws reflect lawlessness, selfishness, and self-gratification. Is this what America's churches are also reflecting?

When we worship purposefully and properly, there is a rearranging of the heavenly (or spiritual) realm above a nation until heaven touches earth over that nation. Heaven is allowed to enter earth in that place of purposeful worship! When we, as worshipers, understand our identity and our purpose, then we can change this nation back to the 'One nation under God' it was established to be.

When our nation is not under God then we can expect the division that we have been experiencing to continue. We say the pledge with these words, "One nation, under God, indivisible." If we are not under God, then we are most definitely a divided nation! To unite the nation, we must put ourselves, as a nation, willingly back under the authority of the ONE TRUE GOD! I believe we can change this nation if we understand the purpose of worship.

Sixteen years ago, the Lord began to download a huge revelation through a book in the Bible. It was right after our daughter, Gabrielle, had died of a brain tumor at the age of six, and three months later, to the day, I was in surgery to remove colon cancer from my body.

To say I was not in the mood or the mind set (I didn't think) to receive such a huge revelation would be an understatement. But sometimes when we are in what we term as our lowest place, is when we are the most devoid of self, and God can give us the most of His presence, and His revelation that can both change us and the nation in which we reside. When I am weak, He is strong.

Day by day I would awaken and arise to meet the Lord and the Holy Spirit in my prayer chair. Each day I was given more instructions and more revelation from verse by verse dissecting of the scriptures. It was the Book of Esther, which I had taught for decades in my life and ministry.

I did not think there was more revelation that I didn't already know or had uncovered. But I was so wrong. I had only scratched the surface. I was instructed to look up every verse! The Spirit of God had me search out the original text in ancient Hebrew verse by verse until I had seen everything He wanted me to see and know in this season of my life. We miss so much when we hurry through anything. We need to learn to slow down and live in the present with God.

One of the greatest revelations that I can apply now to this divine government revelation happened toward the end of the story, when most people, who are preaching, or teaching, or even telling this story stop short.

Once God's people were saved, and the evil Haman was hanged, and a new law was written that gave God's people the right to protect themselves against the old law written, most people stop studying this story. There was so much more about the nation that follows in the last few chapters and verses.

Once Esther's identity changed, (in chapter five she arose on the third day, and put on her own royal robes, dressing herself in her true identity as royalty within the nation, and married the king, becoming not just his queen, but his wife!), then things began to change quickly! Once she became his wife, her level of authority was greatly increased.

She was now united as *one* with the ruler of the nation, and she had his authority through the power of his name. She not only pleaded for the lives of her people, which were a nation within a nation, but through her insistence, a new law was written so they could protect themselves. Finally, the governmental system was set up differently, and God's people, under the leadership of Queen Esther and Mordecai, changed the Persian kingdom!

This is what we can do, when we learn who we are as worshipers and the purpose of worship is established here in America, or in whatever country you reside. Divine government is not set up from Mount Sinai, from the law position, but rather, from Mount Zion, the place and purpose of governmental authority that opens the portal of heaven and brings God's authority to the earth, all through our pure and holy worship!

We have come to Mount Zion! The purpose of worship can change a national government and put God back on the throne within a nation simply by pure and holy, intimate and personal worship!

This is why we must know who we are! It is not about what we do, but rather who we are that can change a nation and put God in His rightful position of power within a nation's borders! That's how powerful and purposeful the timing of you being on the earth, at this time, is!

You were created for such a time as this to help restore and reestablish God's divine governmental plan in the nation that you reside and call home right now! Start worshiping and don't stop until you have opened the portal of heaven and brought the realm of God's kingdom to the earth right where you are!

When we know who we are, then what we do is birthed out of our true eternal identity. This is the way the kingdom of God was set up on the earth. When we try and obey the Lord with our 'doing for Him' based solely upon works, then the works themselves, are simply flesh works.

You can know who you are. You can know your eternal identity. The same action can be accomplished from our

time spent in His presence, ultimately, changing who we are from the inside out. Once that change of heart is made, then all our actions are birthed out of our 'being' instead of our flesh.
The most amazing part of this is the action/work may be exactly the same to the person watching, or receiving the action, but the heart behind the action is known only by the One who created us. Even we do not realize the heart behind what we do, until we are arrested in His presence and made to sit at His feet, then our hearts can be revealed to us!

God demands obedience, but that obedience must be birthed out of a heart that is submitted and obedient to the will of the Father, and not for accolades, or approval, or applause of people. Divine government for this earth realm is established through the purity of our heart of worship. Is it any wonder that many nations, America included in this, have 'flesh' government instead of 'divine' government in action today?

When worship is out of place within the temple of the Lord, then the national government is also out of place, misguided, and, many times, corrupt. We can change this by cleansing our hearts and purifying our minds before God Almighty, and bring back pure, holy, and righteous worship to the throne of grace in our praise and worship!

I don't know about you, but I want our nation to turn back to God for the glory of God. I want to recognize our nation, America, as a true 'one nation under God; in God we trust' nation. I want our government and its laws to reflect righteousness, and not what we, as the church of the living God, have allowed it to become because of our apathetic attitudes within the kingdom of God inside this nation.

You may be thinking, "What can I do as one person, one

voice, to change a nation for God?" If everyone feels that same way then we will do nothing, and eventually, evil will take our nation from us because of our individual voices being silenced. You are not small! You are ONE! You can make a difference but you must push through and use your God given sound wave for His glory and purpose. You can change your family with your ONE voice. You can change your community, your place of employment, your town, place, or city. You can change your local government, your state government, and ultimately, your nation government by finding your voice of influence and using it for God's divine purposeful plan. You can change the nation by making your sound of intercession and worship from right where you are right now!

Will you worship with me with a divine purposeful plan to bring our nation to its knees at the foot of the cross of Jesus? Then we can move our nation back to its rightful place in Zion! Zion is the place of purposeful worship, to put a nation back in divine position for the glory of God! We can do it, one voice at a time. How can we move a nation back to God? We can move one person at a time back into godly position and displace the giants of unbelief, self-focused, self-purposed, self, self, self that has taken the place of our Holy God in this land.

II Timothy 3:1-7 states the condition of our land right now. Read the verses and see if you can see America and even the whole world and its condition stated right in the scriptures.

"*But know this, that in the last days perilous times will come: For men will be lovers of themselves, lovers of money, boasters, proud, blasphemers, disobedient to parents, unthankful, unholy*
Unloving, unforgiving, slanderers, without self-control, brutal, despisers of good,

Traitors, headstrong, haughty, lovers of pleasure rather than lovers of God,
Having a form of godliness but denying its power. And from such people turn away!
For of this sort are those who creep into households and make captives of gullible women loaded down with sins, led away by various lusts,
Always learning and never able to come to the knowledge of the truth."

I could go on, but I think you can see that the condition of the people of the world in this day and age lines up exactly with the verses described as "In the last days". We cannot continue to see this degradation of our society and stay silent any longer. We must find our voices and pray, truly pray, and stand in the gap for our nation. If every person who feels the conviction to pray actually would pray we could turn the nation back to our God!

If you are still not convinced you can make a difference I want to give you one more scripture that clearly defines one of the rolls of the fallen angel of worship, Lucifer. He lost his influence in the throne room when he became lifted up and pride caused his great fall from his heavenly position. Read with me in the Book of Isaiah 14:12-15.

"How you are fallen from heaven,
O Lucifer, son of the morning!
How you are cut down to the ground,
You who weakened the nations!
For you have said in your heart:
'I will ascend into heaven,
I will exalt my throne above the stars of God;
I will also sit on the mount of the congregation
On the farthest sides of the north;
I will ascend above the heights of the clouds,

I will be like the Most High.'
Yet you shall be brought down to Sheol,
To the lowest depths of the Pit."

I want you to look this passage up in your Bible and read on please. Mark the verses and study them all out as this is the fate of Lucifer, the worshiper who fell and took one third of the worshiping angels with him!

For this particular chapter I want to only focus on one phrase within these scriptures. Notice the last line of verse 12 as the statement is made on the time line of after Lucifer has fallen and been cut down to the ground. Notice the next sentence. "YOU WHO WEAKENED THE NATIONS!"

The statement in the scriptures plainly states that Lucifer in his fallen state as Satan has the ability to weaken the nations and in this particular passage is used in the past tense verb. "You who weakened the nations." Satan will do anything in his power to weaken nations and turn entire nations away from the Most High. He stated as Satan that "I will exalt my throne above the stars of God; I will also sit on the mount of the congregation."

When God is not in His proper place within the worship of a nation, then Lucifer, now as the fallen Satan, has exalted his throne and he sits on the mount of the congregation. Our churches and our personal worship sets governments in place; whether it is the dark demonic government led by the fallen angel of worship, Satan, or through Zion, God's divine government can be positioned forever above a nation.

It is up to us, the people of the nation, to continue to push through in worship and intercession to cause God to be enthroned above Satan and his demonic realm. We must push with worship and prayer, divine intercession, causing God to be enthroned on the MOUNT OF THE CONGREGATION of Zion!

Everything Satan knows about ruling and reigning he learned from his position within the throne room of God. We must not allow his fallen knowledge of God's system to continue to turn national government after national government away from the one true God. We must worship until God's government is divinely reset above our nation, and re-position our God in His rightful place above America. One nation under God! One nation under God! One nation under God!

I need you to stand with me, and proclaim, that we are:
One nation under God!
In God we trust!
America is God's nation!
Righteousness prevails within America!
We reverse the curse over and within this nation's borders with our worship and our praise.
Our God reigns in the United States of America!
(If you are from a different nation, then proclaim these same statements of faith over your nation!)

Chapter Nine
Secret Identity

Matthew 6:6, "But you, when you pray, go into your room, and when you have shut your door, pray to your Father who is in the secret place; and your Father who sees in secret will reward you openly."

About a year ago Pastor Jamie Morgan of Life Church invited Harry and me to minister in Williamstown, New Jersey. We had a wonderful time and completely connected with Pastor Jamie and her husband Kurt, and the entire church family. After we returned home I received a book in the mail entitled *Secrets to the Secret Place* by Bob Sorge. I thanked her for sending it to me and promptly lay in on the pile beside my prayer chair. It wasn't that I didn't want to read it; I was very intrigued by it, as the Lord has been dealing with me for a long time about my intimacy with Him.

I wanted to read it but I waited to be still before the Lord. One morning early as I got my cup of coffee and sat down alone with Him while the house was still quiet, I saw the book and heard the Lord say, "Pick it up." So I did.

I opened it up and started reading as I always do from the contents page forward. The Spirit of God arrested me and told me that He was about to download a revelation for my personal secret place with Him. As He guided me I opened my Bible and began to read the above passage of scripture. All of a sudden it was as if the words jumped off the page at me! It read like this, *"But YOU, when YOU pray, go into YOUR room, and when YOU have shut YOUR door, pray to YOUR Father who is in the secret place; and YOUR Father who sees in secret will reward YOU openly."*

Each time the word 'you' or 'your' jumped off the page right into my face! I began to realize that the secret place the Lord has for us, has hidden within it a secret identity of who I am. I saw that my secret identity came from the time I spent in the secret place with Him. I saw that my choice was vital to entering the secret place and it was up to me to decide if I would do what it would take each and every time to access His presence.

My secret identity began to take shape from the secret place. If I wanted more of His presence then I had to learn to access the secret place personally and privately. I had to make several powerful decisions to walk in my secret identity and I had to learn that nothing would last long that was obtained in the secret place. It was like the manna that the Lord provided for the children of Israel. It would only last until the next morning and then they had to go out and gather the manna for that day only.

But me, when I pray . . . hum. I can never access the secret place where my secret identity can be weaved into my being with my first choosing to pray, and not just any prayer . . . anywhere. I had to go into my room and shut my door. Ok, I could do that. I could go into my prayer room, and be in my prayer chair. I had done this for many years. But that was not enough. I had to shut my door.

I felt the Lord begin to guide me. So I closed my eyes in my prayer chair in my prayer room. I saw a circular room in front of me. I knew instinctively that it was the throne room of God's presence within me.

1 Corinthians 6:19 states, "*Or do you not know that your body is the temple of the Holy Spirit who is in you, whom you have from God, and you are not your own?*"

Lord, I know I am the temple of the Holy Spirit and I know

you are in me. I felt Him gently nudge me toward the opening in front of my spirit. As I drew near to this circular throne room within my spirit man I found myself at the threshold of a doorway into the Holy place. I wanted to be inside with Him. I felt Him drawing me, even wooing me to come closer and step on inside the room.

I picked up my foot and stepped over the threshold and I heard the Lord guide me to shut the door behind me. I reached back and leaned against the open door behind me and as I did it gently shut. I had shut my door. All of a sudden I heard the Lord say for me to walk the perimeter of the room. It was circular so I started making my way around the outer realm of the room.

I realized that I had more than one door open. I felt the Lord say to me to shut each door. I had no idea that when I had entered my private room to pray in the past that I had not shut the doors of distraction. I realized the phone was too close in proximity to my prayer chair and each time a message from the myriad of places now that messages can come from the phone would let me know there was a message. Ok, Lord, I see, that is a door of distraction. I reached over and shut off my phone.

As I walked the outskirts of the room, I heard the dryer bell sound that a load of laundry was finished. Without thinking, I rose from my chair and I heard the Spirit of the Lord say, "Shut your door." Another one! I stopped walking around the room and started to pray. "Holy Spirit help me to see the doors that need to be shut in my secret place with you."

The Spirit of God began to guide me around the room until I had shut every door. I felt the Lover of my soul gently touch my chin and pull my eyes up to His. "Now look at Me," I heard Him say and I looked deep in the eyes of the One who loves me more than I will ever be able to fathom the depth of His love. I was lost in His love for a long time. I had finally accessed the secret place of His identity and found my own secret identity within Him.

I will never again try to pretend like I am in the secret place when all of my doors are still wide open. I will take the time to enter the secret place cloaked in my secret prayer identity and each time I will walk the perimeter and make sure every one of my doors is shut. Then I will worship Him the way He deserves to be worshiped . . . with undivided attention and complete secret place identity.

But you, when you pray, won't you step over the threshold of your secret place and make sure every one of your doors are shut. I realized that He does not meet me in the secret place but He *is* the secret place. He is what, who, and where you long to be. He is all in all your secret identity. Don't try to pray without taking the time to access the secret place and find your secret identity within Him.

Let's go together. Close your eyes and step closer. Now lift your foot over the threshold and go on in to His presence, His secret presence. He is a secret for you, not from you. He has hidden Himself right where you can quickly find Him. But it's up to you to shut your doors of distraction and just be with Him for a while, without agenda, or a list of prayers. He's the Lover of your soul, the One who makes you whole. Just worship Him now. See His face and look closely now. Can you see it? There it is . . . your own reflection. Your secret identity is His identity.

Don't be discouraged if the first time you try this "prayer exercise" you have a hard time actually getting to the center of the throne room. It's an exercise and a discipline of your body, soul, and spirit. You must try again and again until you are there! You can be alone with the One who created you, and gave you your identity, your DNA code, your personal cellular frequency! He is calling you to come into His presence but it takes spiritual discipline, which begins first by bringing your flesh under to 'be still' and step out of time for a moment.

You can't expect God to get on your little merry-go-round of fast paced life. You must step out of time for a little while and trust that He is more than capable of causing all things to work together for you, because you love God, and you are called according to His purpose. So relax for a minute and loosen your grip on your 'to do list' today. Step away for a moment with the Lover of your soul. He is gently calling you to come away with Him.

Now let's try it again. Close your eyes and just be still for a while. I can't tell you how long; this is spirit to Spirit, not a math formula. This is a romance of the Spirit so breathe deep and exhale your frustrations, stresses, and timelines. Rest in His presence. He will guide you into all truth.

See the entrance to the throne room right in front of you. There it is. Now step over the threshold. You are in. Don't turn around. Just reach behind you and gently shut your door. He is with you, guiding you, directing you, leading you to be with Him. Walk the perimeter of the circular throne room, and as you see a door open, even a crack, just lean on it with your back and shut your open doors. You are not in time right now; you are in His presence. Rest for a while.

As you circle the throne shut all your doors that are open and keep moving toward Him. Can you see Him on His throne? He is enthroned on your worship. Worship Him. Don't think, don't reason, just worship Him. It's a romance; tell

Him something beautiful about Who He is to you. Don't talk the whole time; just be. Get comfortable being still with Him.

Learning to listen more and talk less in His presence will help you settle and seal your secret identity in His presence. Again this is not a formula; it's a romance of His presence. You will never truly know who you are, until you fully comprehend who He is. I am not saying you will know all of Who He is! We will spend all of eternity and never fully comprehend all of the dimensions of our God and Creator.

He is infinite and so is all of His facets, personalities, abilities, dimensions of dimensions! We are finite. He is infinite. Now wrap your mind around the fact that our infinite Creator loves you beyond anything your mind is capable of comprehending!

Now let's try again. Stand at the entrance of His presence. He deserves your full attention. Step over the threshold. Reach behind you and shut your door. Walk the perimeter of the circular throne room of His presence and shut every one of your doors of distraction. Go to His feet and worship Him.

He will be with you. He will show you more of Who He is and in turn, the more of Him you know, the more of your identity will be sealed and settled within you. This is not a sprint or a relay race. This is personal, private, intimate, and forever.

Your secret identity makes you a 'secret agent' for the King. So come with me. Let us go again. This time you don't need me to take you in. You go on your own and discover more than ever before. You will never need to operate again from the 'tree of knowledge'. You will be able to operate from the 'Tree of Life' from this day forward.

From His presence write a love letter to the Lover of your soul. He deserves for you to pour out your heart before Him without reservation. This is just between the two of you; go ahead and worship Him with your sounds, words, and true secret identity. He has a special name for you, just between lovers. Rest and be still. Learn to listen and accept His love without performance. He adores you.

Chapter Ten
I Am A Worshiper

"I have been crucified with Christ; it is no longer I who live, but Christ lives in me; and the life which I now live in the flesh I live by faith in the Son of God, who loved me and gave Himself for me." Galatians 2:20

Paul made this bold statement of his born again life change as having experienced the crucifixion with Christ. He then stated that it was no longer Paul who was living, but Christ who was living within him. We can say the same thing, but we need to have experienced this moment of dying to our 'self' and dying to our carnal fleshly way of living and thinking.

To be a worshiper of God, I must be hidden inside of Christ to the point that there is nothing left of me. I am totally free from my old sin nature and free to live a sinless, holy, righteous life. This is more than possible; it is absolutely necessary to make the statement, "I am a worshiper!"

This statement is more than a sentence. This statement is more than four words said aloud. This statement is positioning power to life, here on this earth, without the constraints of my old nature of sin dominating my every moment.

I am crucified with Christ. I am dead to my old self with Christ. Christ is resurrected, therefore, I am resurrected to a new life, a new being of freedom from my carnal flesh. I am living heaven on earth with the power to overcome the enemy and my old flesh nature! Jesus gave us that power through the resurrection, and then left us the Holy Spirit (Acts 1:8) to walk out a resurrected lifestyle every moment of every day for the rest of our natural lives!

"I am a worshiper" is a statement of powerful positioning in the kingdom of heaven here on this earth. Ephesians 2:6 states that we have been seated in heavenly places. The past tense verb gives us a perfect picture that, once we have been crucified, and dead to our own flesh and carnal nature, and old things are passed away, and all things have become new, that I am now seated in heavenly places. It is done and finished. My heavenly position has been secured and I am already seated!

My position of power and authority is because of my elevated seating! I am already seated in heavenly places. I am not living my life trying to earn my position. Jesus died and rose from the dead to earn my seat in heavenly places (position of authority) for me. When I accept who He is in my life and I am willing to lay down my carnal flesh nature to walk free of it, then I am immediately seated in heavenly places! Right about now you should be jumping up and down with joy of freedom and positioned power and authority!

Many people say that they are born again, or call themselves Christians, but they have not experienced a conversion of old to new in Christ. Without the experience of Christ within us a statement of being a Christian is said merely out of tradition and religion rather than out of a true relationship with Christ. Many will say that they are Christians simply because they live in America, or have been in church all their lives, or their mama is a Christian.

Truth of a born again experience is hidden in the word *experience*. Knowing Christ is a journey, a lifetime journey of experience with Him. It starts with understanding that we are turning loose of our old nature, our sin nature, and our old carnal fleshly self, and grasping the truth of who He is in our lives.

To state that you are a worshiper means you have given up all other identities apart from your Christ identity. "I am a worshiper" is not in a list of many personas of who you are. Being a worshiper of Christ is the all in all, all-encompassing circle of complete and total life in Christ.

Most people will live their entire lives and never truly experience the freedom of living free from sin, and walking 'dead' to oneself, and being alive forevermore within Christ! Once your identity as a worshiper becomes a reality to you, your daily life will change dramatically. You will hunger for His presence. You will hunger for the secret place where He alone will meet you, and complete you every day.

You can walk with truth and spirit in full operation of your daily life. You are free to live without the constraints of a sin nature. You have put on Christ! You cannot maintain a sin nature and a Christ nature. They are diametrically opposed to each other. You must choose.

I John 3:3-10, "And everyone who has this hope in Him purifies himself, just as He is pure.
Whoever commits sin also commits lawlessness, and sin is lawlessness.
And you know that He was manifested to take away our sins, and in Him there is no sin.
Whoever abides in Him does not sin. Whoever sins has neither seen Him nor known Him.
Little children, let no one deceive you. He who practices righteousness is righteous, just as He is righteous.
He who sins is of the devil, for the devil has sinned from the beginning. For this purpose the Son of God was manifested, that He might destroy the works of the devil.

Whoever has been born of God does not sin, for His seed remains in him; and he cannot sin, because he has been born of God.
In this the children of God and the children of the devil are manifest: Whoever does not practice righteousness is not of God, nor is he who does not love his brother."

I know these are hard verses to wrap your head around so stop trying to get your mind to comprehend this profound truth. Just accept this in your heart where you have the capacity to think beyond your mind's ability. (***As a man thinks in his heart** . . .)* Your spiritual heart has the ability to think beyond your natural brain's ability to conceive and receive truth.

Receive 1 John 3 with your heart's thinking. You have the right and the freedom to walk free from sin forever in Christ. I am reminded of a vision the Lord showed me when I was first beginning to grasp the truth of 'being crucified with Christ."

I was with the Lord, and suddenly He took me up in the Spirit and we were in a cemetery. We were standing right in front of a man's headstone, and I read the man's name, birth date, dash mark, and death date. The Spirit of the Lord said to me, "Hurt this man's feelings. Offend his heart." I was surprised by such a request from the Lord and I didn't respond. I just stood there trying to figure out what the Lord had just said to me, and what my response should be.

Again the Lord said to me, "Hurt his feelings. Say mean things to him." I just stood there trying to process such a command from the Lord. The third time the Spirit of the Lord said to me, "Offend this man. Say hurtful words to him." Finally I responded, "Lord, I can't say a thing to this man that will hurt him. He's dead."

The Lord responded to me, "Exactly. When you are dead enough, no one can hurt your feelings, or offend you, or get you off track from your calling by their words." Immediately I was back in my body, and I knew that I was not 'dead' yet because people's words could still hurt me or get me side tracked. Not anymore though. I know that I am crucified with Christ.

It is my aim to live crucified with Christ. It is no longer I who lives, but Christ who lives in me. When I determine to live crucified, then my flesh and my feelings, and my emotions are not in control of who I am. I can live without sin. I am free; I am free indeed.

Worship is not what I do. Worship is who I am. When my identity as a worshiper was settled and sealed within me, I stopped disqualifying my gift or talent. I stopped criticizing my voice or any other part of my flesh. I am not flesh. I am spirit.

I don't walk by the flesh, but I walk by the spirit. My flesh does not move me. I am a child of God, led by the Spirit of God, which qualifies me to be called a son of God!

This can only happen when I am dead to myself and hidden inside of the only Son of God, Jesus Christ. We live in a society that judges another person, especially when we first meet them, on what they do for a living.

We start conversations with introductions, "How are you? My name is Cheryl Salem." Then a polite and mannerly person will respond and give their name as well. Usually the next question is, "What do you do?" Why? Why would that be the next question after we learn the name of a person?

Why is our identity so wrapped up in what we do? What we do could change tomorrow, but who we are is set in concrete within our beings!

Because in our society our worth is based upon what we do and has very little to do with who we are! This is earth perspective thinking and being. God does not ever qualify us by what we do. In fact, His word makes it clear over and over again that our earthly occupation has nothing to do with our eternal value or worth. But who we are, now there is the real determining factor.

Throughout the Bible, we are told to 'be saved, be healed, be filled with the Holy Spirit, be holy, be righteous', etc. Not one instance does the Bible state that we are to 'do saved, do healed, do filled with the Holy Spirit', etc. Why? Because it is our 'being' that is affected by the eternity of eternities.

It is our *being* that must be submitted and completely turned over to the leading of the Holy Spirit. We are to 'be hidden in Christ.' He does not command us to 'do hidden in Christ.'

Supernatural transformations may not change our occupation, but it most certainly changes the nature of who we are. That's why my heart is to change the way you think about worship from something you *do* into *someone you are*.

You *are* a worshiper, you don't *do* worship. Any musician, or singer, or dancer, or performer can 'do worship' in the traditional sense of the word. But God has not called us to 'do worship'. He has called us to be kings and priests of the most-high God, and in that calling, we become worshipers. In truth, we become worship.

Whether you are on the platform or in a seat in the sanctuary, whether you are in the grocery store line or the drive through window, you are worship. Every thought, action, and deed that happens in your daily life is not works, but a reflection of who you are.

I don't have to think about being nice to people, or loving people, or talking about my Jesus, it's who I am! Is it who you are? It should be. You were created to worship the King of kings. He has made you a king and priest unto our God.

It's who you are, not what you do. So go ahead and say it. Confess it now and every day for the rest of your life. The more you say it, the more you will believe it and walk the confession out every day of your life. I am a worshiper. I am a worshiper. I am a worshiper. It is not what I do; it is who I am. You are a worshiper. It is who you are!

Worshipers Prayer of Surrender

"Let the words of my mouth and the meditation of my heart be acceptable in Your sight, my strength and my redeemer! What can the instrument do apart from the One who is doing the playing? The instrument can do nothing, apart from the One. So, here I am Lord, play me. Make me your melody, Your lyric, Your sound! Let me be the sound through which the world hears and recognizes the very existence of an all- powerful God! Let the world hear through me the sound waves of Your love, Your overpowering strength, Your pure and cleansing streams. Lord, use me, play me as Your instrument of pleasure. Let the sound waves of your presence come forth beckoning, crying out, singing, renewing, reviving, quickening, all who long for You! Let them hear You through me. I have come before You, and I lay myself, this instrument at Your feet. Lord come down from Your holy habitation, reach down, and pick me up, into Your hands. May Your mighty anointed hands; play the sounds of healing and restoration. Play the sounds of Your glory rising and cleansing all who will listen!" I am a woodwind instrument set before You to be played. Without the breath of Your divine presence, no sound of any value or worth can come forth. I am a stringed instrument laid at Your feet. Without Your divine fingers strumming, plucking, running over the reverberations of these yielded strings, no sound can come forth. I am any and all instruments awaiting the glorious and divine touch of Your presence. Without Your touch, I am a clanging cymbal and a sounding brass, a broken and unproductive sound wave that moves no one and goes no where.

Lord, I am Yours. I trust You. I will no longer belong to You part of the time, and myself part of the time. I belong to You. If there is no sound coming from me, then it is the divine Musician who wishes for this silence, not the instrument. This instrument no longer has a will, for I freely give myself, my will, my mind, my body, my instrument to my divine Creator.

May the light of your glory be seen in me. May the sound of Your presence be heard through me. I am Yours and You are mine. This is My Beloved's song, an eternal love song, but only those who are washed clean by the blood of the Lamb can hear it. Can you hear it? It is the sound of the redeemed crying loudly…even so, "Come, Lord Jesus!"
And the Bridegroom says, "I am coming quickly."
And the Bride says, "Come, Lord, Jesus."
And the Bridegroom says, "I am coming soon."
And the Bride says, "Come, Lord, Jesus."
And the Bridegroom says, "Behold! It is finished; I am coming."
And he Bride says, "Even so! Come, Lord, Jesus!"

"This is trash. It was trash talk when it was first said and it has no more power over me. I am not what these words have said about me. I command any evil words ever spoken over me- every word that I can remember, and those I have forgotten . . . the words I heard, and the words I didn't hear to all come to their end today. None of these words have power over me, or my future in the name of Jesus. I am what God says I am. I am who God says I am. I believe my Creator, the One who designed me, is the only One with power in my life and future. I will say what God's word says about me and I will never again speak an evil word against myself nor will I ever again agree with someone who speaks evil against me in the name of Jesus Christ, my Lord and Savior, Amen!"

Prayer of Salvation

If you have never made Jesus the Lord of your life, or if you would like to re-dedicate your life to Him, please pray this prayer of salvation.

Heavenly Father, I come to You admitting that I am a sinner. Right now, I choose to turn away from sin and I ask You to cleanse me of all unrighteousness. I believe that Your Son, Jesus, died on the cross to take away my sins. I also believe that He rose again from the dead so that I might be forgiven of my sins and be made righteous through faith in Him. I call upon the name of Jesus Christ to be the Lord and Savior of my life. Jesus, I choose to follow You and I ask that You fill me with the power of the Holy Spirit. I declare right now that I am a child of God! I am free from sin and full of the righteousness of God. I am saved, in Jesus' name. Amen.

Please contact us to let us know you prayed this prayer!

Salem Family Ministries
PO Box 1595
Cathedral City, CA 92234
www.salemfamilyministries.org

Please include your prayer requests
and comments when you write.

About the Author

Cheryl Salem walked the runway to become Miss America 1980, despite what appeared to be all odds stacked against her. A horrific car crash resulting in a physical handicap and over 100 stitches in her face, were no match for what God had planned for her life. Through childlike faith in Him, she overcame the obstacles and eventually took the crown in Atlantic City! She has used this distinction as a springboard to launch the Gospel into churches, conferences, and many television appearances. According to Cheryl, "None of these things would be possible, if not for my Jesus."

In 1985, Cheryl married the love of her life, Harry Salem II. Harry and Cheryl Salem travel the world ministering the gospel, telling people that Jesus loves them and that He is returning soon! Their lives revolve around seeking the Lord and where He would have them go. Two by two they travel, loving God's people, living and moving in His anointing.

In 1999, Harry and Cheryl endured the loss of their 6-year-old daughter, Gabrielle. As they boldly took steps of faith to overcome the agonizing pain of Gabrielle's death, they ask God to restore them and for souls to come into His kingdom. God has restored the Salem family and because of His mighty anointing, the altars have been full!

Harry and Cheryl are committed to leading godly lives as an example to others. Roman has married a beautiful young lady, Stephanie, and she has become their daughter-in-love. Healing and restoration has come full circle to the Salem family with the miracle birth of Roman and Stephanie's daughter, Mia Gabrielle and son, Roman Jr.

Harry Salem III continues in the family ministry as he has done since he was a child. He has completed his doctorate in Theology, while Roman and Stephanie are ministering as a couple to both youth and adult services across the country. Harry III, Roman and Stephanie minister with Harry and Cheryl in the Salem Family Ministries events.

Together, Harry and Cheryl have written over 35 books and produced numerous music and ministry CDs to help enable believers to not only overcome but to excel in their Christian lives.

They love people and they love pouring themselves out because God's immense mercy, grace, and love keep them filled up in return.

The Spirit of God is flowing through Cheryl in an amazing way as He leads her to minister in a prophetic manner that involves a flow of music and teaching that is sung, instead of spoken. After surviving and overcoming cancer three times she believes that her call to rebuild and restore worship God's way is the mantle she will fulfill throughout the rest of her life.

Cheryl is a worshiper above all else. She ministers to ladies events across the country, encouraging women to reach their godly potential, but her main objective and central focus for Salem Family Ministries is to take Harry and Cheryl's unique, tag-team style of ministry into churches and gatherings all over this world, going out two by two, to reach families one by one for God's glory! (Luke 10:1-2)

Cheryl Salem

Books by Harry and Cheryl Salem

**I Am A Worshiper Workbook*

**We Who Worship*

**We Who Worship Workbook*

**Rebuilding the Ruins of Worship*

**Rebuilding the Ruins of Worship Workbook*

**Tones of the Throne Room*

**Tones of the Throne Room Workbook*

**The Sound of the Spirit*

**Age of Mystery*

**The Rise of an Orphan Generation: Longing for a Father*

**Two Becoming One*

**Don't Kill Each Other! Let God Do It!*

**From Mourning to Morning*

**From Grief to Glory*

Distractions from Destiny

**Obtaining Peace – A 40-Day Prayer Journal*

**Entering Rest – Be Still – A 40-Day Journey into the Presence of God*

The Presence of Angels in Your Life

Overcoming Fear – A 40-Day Prayer Journal

**A Bright Shining Place - The Story of a Miracle*

Speak the Word Over Your Family for Finances

Speak the Word Over Your Family for Healing

Speak the Word Over Your Family for Salvation

The Choice is Yours

Being #1 at Being #2

For Men Only

A Royal Child

The Mommy Book

Abuse ... Bruised but not Broken

You Are Somebody

**EBooks available at salemfamilyministries.org*

To order these products or to submit a prayer request or praise report, Please vist us at www.salemfamilyministries.org

We would love to hear from you. There are many ways to stay connected with us. You can receive our newsletter by giving us your email address through our web site. It's free and easy.

Salem Family Ministries
P. O. Box 1595
Cathedral City, CA 92234
www.salemfamilyministries.org

Like our page on Facebook
Salem Family Ministries

Subscribe to our YouTube channel
Salem Family Ministries

Connect through my Twitter
or Periscope account
Cheryl Salem @cherylsalem1980